CONTENTS

CW01499207

ILLUSTRATION LIST

THE BATTLE OF
TANGA 1914

Battles & Campaigns

A series of illustrated battlefield accounts covering the classical period through to the end of the twentieth century, drawing on the latest research and integrating the experience of combat with intelligence, logistics and strategy.

Series Editor

Hew Strachan, Chichele Professor of the History of War
at the University of Oxford

Published

William Buckingham, *Arnhem 1944*
David M. Glantz, *Barbarossa*
Michael K. Jones, *Bosworth 1485*
Martin Kitchen, *The German Offensives of 1918*
M.K. Lawson, *The Battle of Hastings 1066*
Tim Travers, *Gallipoli 1915*

Commissioned

Ross Anderson, *The East African Front 1914–18*
Stephen Conway, *The Battle of Bunker Hill 1775*
Brian Farrell, *The Defence & Fall of Singapore 1941–42*
Martin Kitchen, *El Alamein 1942–43*
Marc Milner, *The Battle of the Atlantic 1939–1945*
John Andreas Olsen, *Operation Desert Storm*
Michael Penman, *Bannockburn 1314*
Matthew C. Ward, *Quebec 1759*

THE BATTLE OF
TANGA 1914

ROSS ANDERSON

TEMPUS

First published 2002

PUBLISHED IN THE UNITED KINGDOM BY:
Tempus Publishing Ltd
The Mill, Brimscombe Port
Stroud, Gloucestershire GL5 2QG

PUBLISHED IN THE UNITED STATES OF AMERICA BY:
Tempus Publishing Inc.
2 Cumberland Street
Charleston, SC 29401

British Library Cataloguing in Publication Data.
A catalogue record for this book is available from the British Library.

ISBN 0 7524 2349 5

Typesetting and origination by Tempus Publishing.
Printed in Great Britain by Midway Colour Print, Wiltshire

Cover illustration: Taking cover near Longido (Imperial War Museum, Q45730)

MAPS

ABBREVIATIONS

ACH Collection of Ms Ann Crichton-Harris.

BA/MA Bundesarchiv/Militärarchiv, von Lettow-Vorbeck Papers, N 103/116.

Deppe Deppe, Ludwig, *Mit Lettow-Vorbeck durch Afrika*, Berlin: Verlag August Scherl, 1919.

GR Collection of Mr Gerald Rilling.

IWM Wapshare Imperial War Museum, Department of Documents, Wapshare Papers.

IWM Imperial War Museum, Photograph Archive. Print numbers are shown opposite each reference.

King-Hall King-Hall, Adm Sir H.G., *Naval Traditions and Memories*, London: 1926.

Patience Patience, Kevin, *Königsberg A German East African Raider*, Bahrein: Zanzibar Publications, 1997.

PRO Public Record Office, CAB 45/7.

RHQ QLR Regimental Headquarters, The Queen's Lancashire Regiment.

SANDF Documentation Directorate, South African National Defence Force. Print numbers are shown opposite each reference.

ACKNOWLEDGEMENTS

The research and writing of this book has been greatly assisted by a number of people and institutions. I would particularly like to thank Professor Hew Strachan, firstly as my doctoral supervisor and latterly as Series Editor, for his incisive comments and suggestions on this work and the East African campaign in general. Generously, he also made a number of rare and difficult to obtain sources available for my extended use. Dr Kent Fedorowich kindly read the draft manuscript and made a number of useful and pertinent comments. Additionally, he provided me with valuable research material and leads from his own studies.

The trustees of the Imperial War Museum enabled me to consult the extensive collections of papers in their care. I thank them for permission to quote from the papers of and reproduce photographs belonging to Lt-Col. Sir Richard Wapshare. Furthermore, I gratefully acknowledge Vice Admiral Sir Norman King's permission to publish extracts from the diary of his father, Sir Norman King, as well as to reproduce photographs from his collection. The museum's Photographic Archive has allowed the publication of a number of photographs. The Public Record Office has been extremely important in providing material, including pictures, and I must thank its staff for their assistance. Crown copyright material is reproduced with permission of Her Majesty's Stationery Controller.

The Bodleian and Rhodes House Libraries of the University of Oxford gave me access to their vast and important collections. In Germany, the Bundesarchiv-Militärarchiv in Freiburg has been most accommodating and enabled me to consult its invaluable documentary and photographic holdings. The librarians and staff of the British Library, the University of Glasgow Library and the National Army Museum have all been most efficient and helpful. The Documentation Directorate of the South African National Defence Force has allowed me to consult its important collections and to reproduce photographs from its archive. Regimental Headquarters, The Queen's Lancashire Regiment, has been very helpful in providing access to the records of the Loyal North Lancashire Regiment as well as allowing me to reproduce pictures from its holdings.

In North America, Ms Ann Crichton-Harris has been particularly enthusiastic and supportive of the book and I owe her many thanks. She kindly allowed me to quote from her book, *Seventeen Letters to Tatham*, as well as using her numerous photographs of Tanga. Similarly, Mr Gerald Rilling's long-standing and deep knowledge of the area and its history were most helpful in clarifying a number of issues. He also provided valuable bibliographic advice and a number of pictures from his private collection. Mr Brian Garfield has shared the results of his extensive researches into the campaign through a number of stimulating discussions.

I must also mention Mr Kevin Patience, who provided useful advice on naval operations and local conditions. He also allowed me to reproduce a number of photographs from his book *Königsberg,* for which I am most grateful. Finally, I would like to thank my publisher, Mr Jonathan Reeve, Ms Joanna Lincoln, and the staff of Tempus for their help in bringing the projection to completion. Finally, my family deserves the greatest thanks for their unflagging and patient support of my lengthy researches.

1

INTRODUCTION

The battle of Tanga, fought between 2 and 5 November 1914, has become one of the best-known events of one of the more obscure campaigns of the First World War. Although dwarfed in scale by the huge battles being waged in Europe, Tanga was important as it marked the beginning of a colonial adventure that would ultimately last over four years and would involve much of East Africa. It was also an early example of the lack of consistency and thoroughness in British strategic planning that was to carry on through the failures at the Dardanelles and Mesopotamia. The battle also exposed major limitations in the existing cabinet system and in the machinery of providing military advice to the Government, including the need for the unified direction of operations world-wide. Finally, it underlined the lack of joint planning between the military services and weaknesses in the Indian Army's operational readiness. All in all, Tanga was an unmitigated fiasco.

This is important as during the first two years of the war, British arms suffered a number of miscues and failures, particularly outside Europe. Despite the need for visible successes, it is noteworthy that many of fundamental errors made at Tanga were repeated a few months later at the Dardanelles.[1] There seems to have been no mechanism either to learn or disseminate the lessons from past errors; hence they were repeated at great cost in lives and suffering. If Tanga exposed the many weaknesses in the British war machinery of the early war period, virtually no improvements came out of it. Perhaps East Africa was too far from home and of insufficient strategic value to merit greater scrutiny or interest. Equally, military and political leaders seemed unwilling to subject themselves and their departments to critical self-analysis, with the result that future and even greater disasters awaited them.

To Imperial Germany, the battle was of much less significance as their colony *Deutsch-Ostafrika* – German East Africa – had been cut off at the outbreak of war and their strategic focus remained resolutely on the main theatres of war. However, at a local, colonial level, the barely submerged tensions between the civil and military powers were brought to a head by the fighting and were never satisfactorily resolved. On the other hand, success brought renewed confidence to their troops, known as the *Schutztruppe*, and their commander, Lt-Col. Paul von Lettow-Vorbeck. It also confirmed his aggressive military policy and gave him the upper hand over the governor. It was not all one way, as the battle also highlighted a number of important weaknesses in the military organisation that would require resolution in the subsequent months. Nevertheless, Germany gained a useful, if strategically limited, victory at Tanga.

It was perhaps unsurprising that, apart from the immediate participants, Tanga was little known at the time. By the end of October 1914, with the heavy fighting at Ypres following the heavy losses in the frontier battles and the counter-attack on the Marne, British attention was focused on France and Flanders, as was much of the German offensive effort. Germany was also engaged in heavy fighting against the Russians in Poland while the Austro-Hungarians were occupied in Galicia and Serbia. Furthermore, Turkey had entered the war on the side of the Central Powers, forcing Britain to rush troops to Egypt and the Persian Gulf. These moves added emphasis on the Mediterranean and Middle Eastern theatres, leaving Africa far behind in importance.

At sea, the British Royal Navy continued to contain the German High Sea Fleet in its North Sea bases but had not been able to bring it to the expected decisive battle. In the Pacific Ocean, Admiral von Spee had defeated a British squadron in the battle of the Coronel and was making his way to the South Atlantic. Elsewhere, the numerically superior Royal Navy, in conjunction with the French, Russians and Japanese, was hunting down the remaining German surface raiders in an attempt to secure the vital sea lanes from interference.

In this context, it seems hardly surprising that a small and rather motley convoy consisting of one light cruiser, an armed auxiliary and twelve troopships was making its way across the Indian Ocean largely unnoticed. Sailing from India, its destination was the East African coast where it would bring the war to the obscure and little developed colony of German East Africa. This force, carrying two brigades of the Indian Army, was due to launch an ill-conceived and badly planned offensive that was intended to seize the biggest colony of the German Empire. Few would have guessed that this expedition would start a campaign which would last until after the Armistice had been concluded in November 1918 and would range across much of East Africa.

Public knowledge of Tanga would have to await the end of the war. The first published account of the battle came out in 1920, with the German commander's book *My Reminiscences of East Africa*.[2] Written entirely from memory during his return journey to Germany, Lettow gave a vivid and brisk account of the entire campaign, including Tanga. Although he did not have his diaries returned until after publication, the book is an accurate guide to his own actions, although it is less reliable when dealing with others. With Lettow's reputation as a chivalrous and gallant commander who was never defeated, it became a minor classic and has been used almost exclusively as the full account of German operations at Tanga. But, it should be remembered that it was written in light of Germany's humiliating defeat and was seeking to emphasise the loyalty and steadfastness of the colonial troops. Furthermore, Lettow sought to put his own views on the conduct of the campaign forward, as he was still engaged in a bitter dispute with his former governor, Dr Heinrich Schnee, who had published his own memoirs in 1919.[3]

The great influence of Lettow may also be attributed to the fact that he wrote in English as well as German. This easy accessibility and lack of alternate sources helped to stamp his version as definitive. But, in 1958, his loyal former staff officer and later *Reichsarchivist*, Capt. Ludwig Boell, produced an extensive and authoritative account of the campaign called *Die Operationen in Ostafrika*.[4] This work was based on official documents and maps, many of which were destroyed by bombing in April 1945, while Boell had consulted extensively with the British official historians prior to the outbreak of the Second World War. It is an informative and fair account that supplements Lettow considerably, but unfortunately has been little used.

On the British side, an accurate assessment of Tanga was much slower in appearing. During the war, the Government deliberately suppressed news of the failure as it feared its impact on public opinion. Thereafter, interest centred on the main theatres of war and the enormous national sacrifices made. In the postwar years, one officer tried to publish an account of the battle, but was prevented from doing so, as it was considered unhelpful for ongoing reforms in the Indian Army.[5] Although it was mentioned in a number of personal memoirs published during the 1920s and '30s, it was not until 1941 that volume one of the British Official History, *Military Operations – East Africa*, appeared in print.[6] As expected, it covered the battle in considerable detail, but gave only cursory treatment to the naval and political background. Furthermore, as an official publication, it was reluctant to criticise individuals too openly, apart perhaps from the failed commander. The history was also launched at an unfortunate time as public interest was naturally centred on surviving and winning the Second World War.

The next significant stage was the publication of the frank and outspoken memoirs of Col. Richard Meinertzhagen, *Army Diary*, in 1960.[7] This work, by an intelligence staff officer, provided an insight into British operations that criticised senior officers and many units heavily. The author's observations, which largely agreed with the comments in Lettow's work and the Official History, were taken as being an entirely accurate picture of the British military effort of the period. Consequently, they have been cited almost as extensively as Lettow's. There is a *caveat*, however, as Meinertzhagen has become a controversial figure with suspicions that his typewritten diaries were possibly amended with the benefit of hindsight. Nevertheless, his account remains an important source, if used with care and correlated with externally verifiable facts. It should also be borne in mind that while both Lettow and Meinertzhagen were present, both authors missed large segments of the engagement and personally witnessed only a relatively small fragment of the battle.

It was not until the 1960s that a number of popular accounts of the war began to emerge. Charles Miller, Brian Gardner and Leonard Mosley all wrote on the campaign, covering Tanga in some detail, but apart from Miller none made use of

Boell's account.[8] Several years later, in the mid-1960s, the Public Record Office made the British First World War files available to the public and, contrary to expectations, they contained a considerable amount of material on Tanga. At about the same time, both the Lettow and Boell papers were deposited in the *Bundesarchiv/Militärarchiv* in Freiburg for preservation. Each collection contains a large quantity of excellent material that has remained largely untouched over the years despite its obvious importance.

Ironically, it was a novel in 1982 by William Boyd, *An Ice Cream War*, that did the most to popularise the battle and the East African campaign.[9] This book, while well written and an excellent story, was never intended to provide a detailed historical account of the fighting. Nevertheless, to many, it represents the public face of the campaign. The next flurry of activity came in the mid-1980s when authors such as Edwin Hoyt, Byron Farwell and Lawrence James wrote upon the war in Africa, but their accounts are based on similar sources and none conducted any original research.[10] It was not until Hew Strachan's magisterial study, *The First World War: To Arms*, was published in 2001 that the war in Africa was given its proper context and relevance.[11]

This account will try to build on the above foundations and provide a balanced account of the battle of Tanga. Before doing so, it will also examine the strategic and political background to the conflict and describe the confused manner in which it came to fruition. It will look at how the pressures of war and the inadequacies of the British military planning process enabled the aims of the expedition to expand greatly beyond its means. Of particular interest, will be the process by which the controversial truces were instigated, partially accepted and then ultimately rejected just prior to the commencement of the battle. The pressures on Indian resources and the delays in the sending of the expedition will be briefly explored as will the inability of the two services to co-ordinate their efforts in a smooth and effective manner. On the German side, the study will consider the relative lack of strategic importance of German East Africa as well as the effects of the effective isolation of the colonial administration from the Imperial Government. It will touch upon pre-war planning for the defence of the colony and how the new commander of the *Schutztruppe* tried to overturn them. This will develop into an overview of the increasingly serious clash of views between the civil and military leaders that resulted in confused responses to British aggression.

The development of both sides' local colonial forces and the British failure to use them effectively will be brought into focus. This will be followed by a description of the events around the landings, leading into a detailed narrative of the battle itself. This will lead into an epilogue that puts the fighting at Tanga in perspective for future campaigns. Finally, conclusions about the conception, planning and execution of the expedition will be drawn together with comments on the performance of the two sides.

2

THE STRATEGIC SITUATION
IN AUGUST 1914

At the outbreak of war, the commitment of the BEF to France notwithstanding, Britain retained its traditional concerns for the command of the seas. In the years leading up to 1914, the Admiralty had followed a programme of withdrawing its best ships to home waters in order to counter the growing threat of the German High Sea Fleet in the North Sea. The corollary of this policy was that the more remote stations were left with ageing and second-rate vessels. Such ships were deemed adequate to deal with the principal expected opposition in the form of the German overseas cruiser force. The bulk of their naval power, the East Asiatic Squadron, was based at Tsingtau, with two light cruisers in the Caribbean and another stationed at Dar-es-Salaam. They also possessed a considerable number of merchant ships that could be converted into auxiliary cruisers with relatively little effort.[1]

If the main clash of British and German naval might was expected in European waters, the other stations were far from being insignificant. As the world's leading trading nation, Britain's position depended on the ocean lanes being kept free from threat. This was not only for sound commercial reasons, but also for food imports and, once war had broken out, for the unimpeded movement of men and material from the far-flung corners of the Empire. In this context, even a single enemy warship could wreak considerable havoc and damage on British interests if left undisturbed. Furthermore, it was known that the Germans intended to use their cruisers to raid commerce and, given the immenseness of the oceans, it would be difficult to track their ships down and destroy them. A particular area of weakness was the waters of the Indian and Pacific Oceans where relatively formidable German naval forces could easily swoop onto the vital shipping moving between Australia, New Zealand, India and the Suez Canal. The East Asiatic Squadron possessed two new armoured cruisers, the *Scharnhorst* and *Gneisenau*, together with three light cruisers, the *Emden*, *Nürnberg* and *Leipzig*. While East Africa had only the light cruiser *Königsberg*, it was very modern and fast. Together, such a force posed a considerable threat to seaborne trade and the all-important troop convoys destined for Europe.[2]

1. SMS *Königsberg.*

2. HMS *Hyacinth.*

On the other hand, the British Cape of Good Hope Squadron, commanded by Rear Admiral Herbert King-Hall, comprised three old light cruisers, the *Hyacinth*, *Astraea* and *Pegasus*. All were slower than the *Königsberg* and none by themselves was a match for the former's guns, although acting as a squadron they were strong enough to sink their opponent. However, responsible for an area of sea ranging from St Helena in the Atlantic to Zanzibar in the Indian Ocean, such a tiny force depended on being in the right place at the right time if it were to have any chance of success. Further north at Bombay, Rear Admiral Sir Richard Peirse's East Indies Squadron held an old battleship, the *Swiftsure*, two light cruisers, the *Dartmouth* and *Fox*, and three sloops. But he too had an enormous area to protect with three key focal points: Aden, and the waters south of Ceylon and Singapore; all of which were critical to shipping. His ships were too far from East Africa to be immediately effective against the *Königsberg* while he had to be prepared for a swoop into his waters by the East Asiatic Squadron.[3]

German East Africa was an unlikely concern for the British as it had been a relatively recent addition to the *Reich*, having only been absorbed as a protectorate in 1892. Since then, Europeans had thinly settled it with the overwhelming majority of the population being African. A tropical country with its northern border on the Equator, it was enormous in size being one and half times the area of metropolitan Germany. It extended for some 700 miles north to south and about 600 miles east to west. In 1914, it had a population of over 7.5 million Africans, 14,000 Indians and over 5,300 Germans – this compared with nearly 7 million Africans,

3. HMS *Astraea*.

4. HMS *Pegasus*.

28,000 Indians and 6,000 Europeans in British East Africa and Uganda.[4] Economically, it was hardly developed and imperial loans to the colony dwarfed its income. Two important railways, the Usambara railway in the north and the Central Railway in the centre of the colony, had been completed by war's outbreak, but the respective costs of 25 million and 111 million marks remained largely outstanding.[5] Like its British counterparts that surrounded it to the north and south, German East Africa was hardly a rich prize to be plucked away at the first opportunity; rather it was a huge tropical expanse with considerable potential, but little present economic or military value.

As the July crisis approached its climax, the British Admiralty took a number of steps to prepare for war. One of these was to order Admiral King-Hall to despatch his ships to Dar-es-Salaam and to shadow the *Königsberg*, and, if war were to break out, to sink it.[6] Immediately diverted from their planned cruise towards Mauritius, the squadron set north towards German East Africa. Their fuel situation was unfavourable as they were unable to replenish at Madagascar and the Admiralty had insisted on the use of lower grade Natal coal rather than the more effective Welsh variety. This had the dual effect of reducing the speed available and of fouling the boilers more quickly.[7] This was to have important effects on the chase for the German raider.

The German colony was well aware of the growing threat of war, having received wireless and cable reports about the growing crisis in Europe. This was reinforced by the realisation that the British were delaying the messages that were transmitted via the undersea cables that came ashore at Zanzibar. On the last day of July, the governor held a conference of his main advisors to discuss military preparations. He

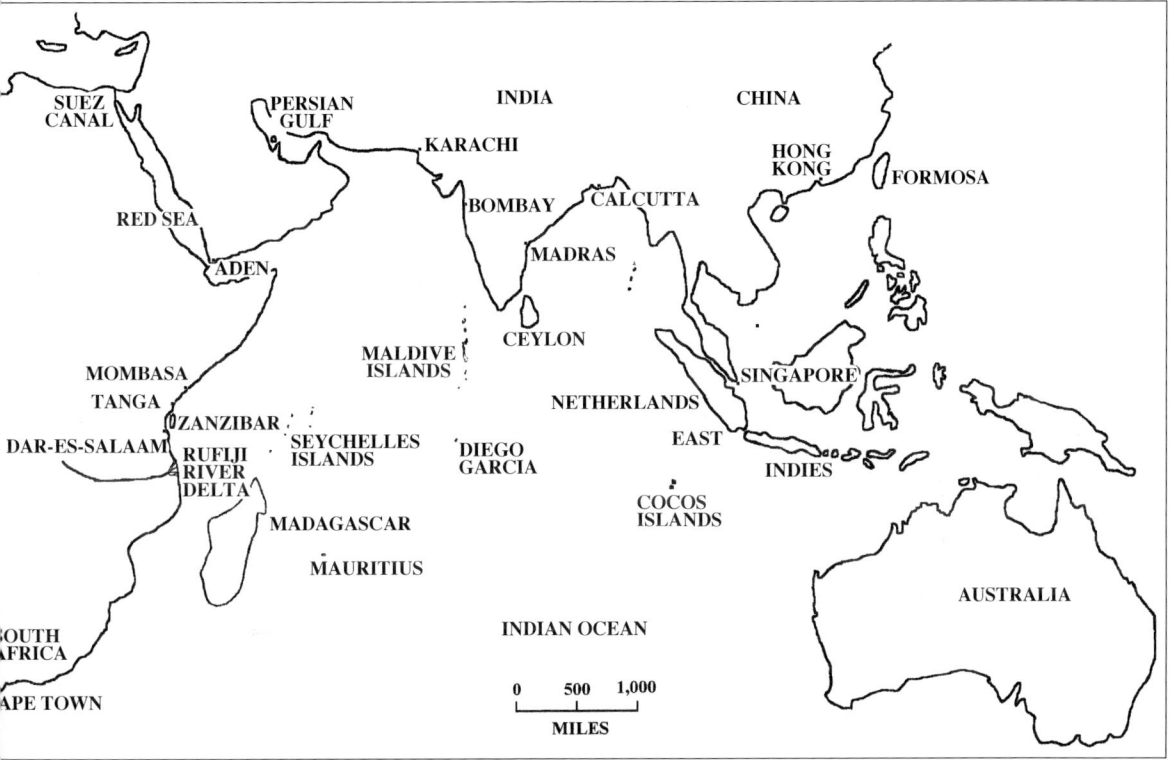

Map 1. East Africa and the Indian Ocean.

decided to implement the pre-war plan of not defending coastal areas that could be shelled from ships and to make preparations to deny the harbour and sink the floating dock. At the same time the *Königsberg* would leave for sea so as to escape any blockade.[8] The importance of this meeting was underlined by a midday warning from a steamer that the British Cape Squadron was heading towards Dar-es-Salaam from Zanzibar. Acting promptly, the cruiser finished its final preparations and slipped its moorings at 1630 hours; it was to be a timely move.[9]

The *Königsberg* was acting in strict accordance with its pre-war orders, that of commerce raiding. The German overseas naval strategy had recognised British material superiority and sought to avoid its strength by providing a force of fast ships able to attack and disrupt the all-important shipping lanes. These cruisers were to be supported by a number of colliers that would draw supplies of coal from pre-positioned stockpiles accumulated in neutral ports. This strategy, known as *Kreuzerkrieg*, would seek to hit the British where they were weakest and disrupt their commercial maritime power. As such, the *Königsberg* had instructions to put to sea as soon as war threatened so as to patrol the Indian Ocean approaches that led to the Red Sea.[10]

Reaching the enemy coastline on the afternoon of 31 July, the first of King-Hall's squadron, the *Pegasus*, sighted the *Königsberg* just after it left harbour. The other two ships closed on either flank and took up position. However, by building up maximum steam and then a sharp reversal of course followed by a turn south,

Looff, commanding the German cruiser, was able to shake the shadowing ships. The superior speed of the *Königsberg* coupled with the British shortage of coal meant that the pursuers were soon left behind.[11] The interception of the sole surface raider had failed at the critical moment for the want of several knots of speed and better fuel. Now faced with tracking down a single ship in the vastness of the Indian Ocean, the British admiral decided that he had to cover his main base at Cape Town, where the German gunboat *Eber* had escaped from the dockyard on 30 July. Accordingly, he sent the *Hyacinth* back, leaving the remaining two ships in East African waters. Further north, Admiral Peirse was having similar concerns about the *Königsberg*, but was unable to despatch any of his warships before its disappearance. That ship now posed a definite menace to the trade routes off Ceylon, while von Spee's squadron had broken out of port and threatened Singapore. The naval situation now appeared perilous as the Germans were capable of concentrating a force of superior speed and firepower virtually anywhere against the vulnerable trade routes.[12] It would also affect the timing of the planned operations against German East Africa quite considerably.

BRITISH POLICY

Following the expiration of the British ultimatum on 4 August, the Cabinet met repeatedly to determine initial policy for the war. While the despatch of the British Expeditionary Force to France and the mobilisation and deployment of the fleet were largely in accordance with pre-war plans, other operations around the world were placed under political scrutiny. On 5 August, the secretary to the Committee for Imperial Defence (CID), Capt. Maurice Hankey, persuaded the prime minister, Henry Herbert Asquith, to set up a new sub-committee of the CID to deal with overseas operations. Rather ponderously entitled 'The Joint Naval and Military Committee for the Consideration of Combined Operations in Foreign Territory', it drew on an *ad hoc* grouping of experts from various Whitehall departments and was charged with:

> The Object of the Committee is to decide what objectives can be assigned to joint operations with a view to produce a definite effect on the result of the war.
>   Having decided the broad lines of any joint operations, the Committee will submit their proposals to the Cabinet; and, in the case of such proposals as may be approved, will work out the details as far as may be necessary.[13]

Meeting on same day as its authorisation, the Offensive Sub-Committee recommended action against a number of German overseas possessions, ranging from the destruction of wireless stations in the Pacific Ocean to the attacking of the larger colonies. Underlying its deliberations was the principle that the maintenance of world-wide naval supremacy was of fundamental importance; its conclusion concerning East Africa reflected this concern:

> The Sub-Committee submit to HM Government their opinion that an expedition should be sent from India against Dar-es-Salaam. They believe by this means the Admiralty arrangements for the protection of commerce would be facilitated by the reduction of the *point d'appui* of the German naval forces off the coast of East Africa, and that by thus taking the offensive the defence of British possessions in East Africa would be guaranteed.[14]

On 6 August, the Offensive Sub-Committee met again and made the further recommendation that a force of some four battalions would be sufficient for the proposed operations against Dar-es-Salaam. It also added a request for a further two battalions to be sent to support the Colonial Government in British East Africa against any possible unrest.[15] The proposals were accepted in principle by the politicians and then sent back to the various ministries for action.[16] Given the time available and the focus on Europe, it is apparent that very little detailed planning for this venture was conducted and possible German responses do not appear to have been considered.[17] Indeed, the War Office was not even involved in the planning, and leadership of the operation devolved onto the India Office with support from the Admiralty.[18]

This lack of co-ordination was to prove critical to the execution of the Sub-Committee's grand designs. In the first meeting, the majority of members were senior officers who happened to be available at the time and who lacked executive authority to carry out the plans. While both the Director of Military Operations and the Admiralty's Chief of the War Staff attended subsequent meetings, the former had nothing to do with the planning and the latter had a number of other, heavy commitments with which to deal. Indeed, the driving force behind the despatch of Indian forces to East Africa and Mesopotamia turned out to be Gen. Sir George Barrow, the Military Secretary at the India Office. Barrow was a retired officer whose principal function was advising the Secretary of State for India on military matters. He had neither the authority nor the staff to supervise military operations, responsibility for which rested with the Viceroy and Commander-in-Chief, India. However, in the heady days of 1914, his proximity to the seat of power, and his drive and determination would greatly influence coming events. In this, he was aided by ministerial enthusiasm for overseas ventures and over-confidence in British ability.

If the overworked naval and military staffs failed to scrutinise the Sub-Committee's recommendations in sufficient detail, rivalry between the civilian ministries also played their part. The shortcomings of the existing cabinet system are well known, but lack of detailed policy co-ordination between the Foreign,

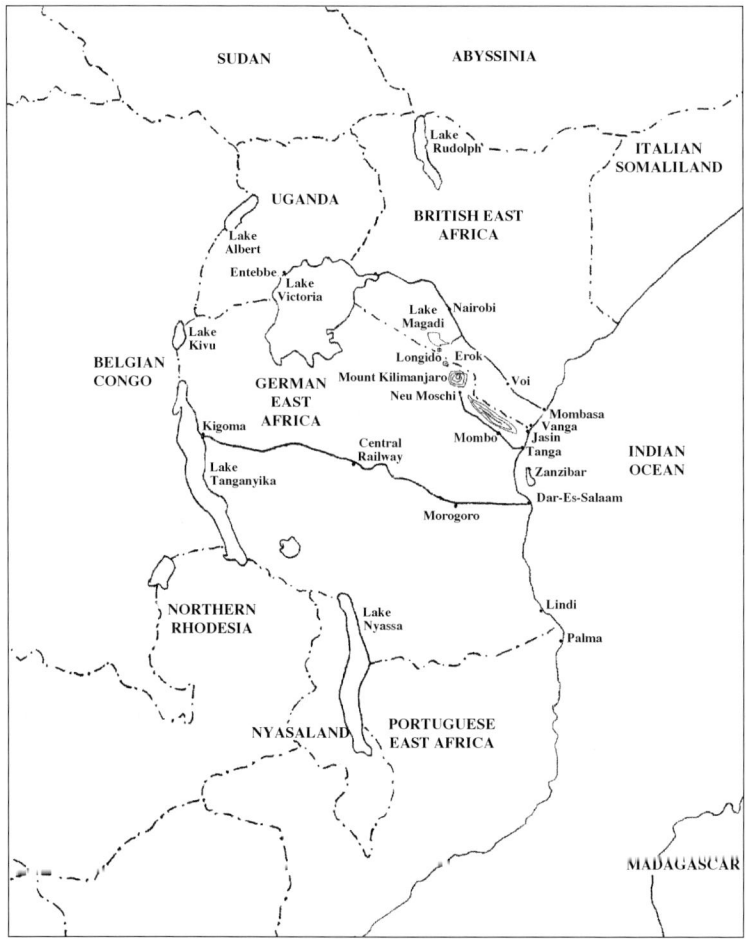

Map 2. East Africa August 1914.

Colonial and India Offices hindered preparations at various stages. The Cabinet system of the day was quite unprepared for the complex demands of modern warfare and departments were content to run along peacetime lines.

The Cabinet's approval in principle of the Offensive Sub-Committee's findings was initially based on the sound strategical principles of protecting the imperial concentration in the main theatre and the security of overseas trade routes. All subsidiary operations were intended to deny the enemy the use of its foreign bases and means of communications without detracting from the main theatre of war. In practical terms this meant the destruction of the German system of wireless and cable links as well as eliminating their coaling facilities and overseas ports. This policy could be largely achieved through a combination of naval action, amphibious raids and pressure on neutral powers. What it did not require was the conquest of substantial inland territories or the commitment of large bodies of troops.[19]

Also attractive was the fact that such a strategy would help to allay allies' fears about British expansionism. In fact, the British Government had specifically ruled out acquiring territories for the purposes of imperial expansion, stating that all permanent decisions would be subject to any post-war peace conference.[20] However, this high-minded declaration did not rule out the conquest of enemy colonies, as such prizes could be useful negotiating pieces.[21] It also recognised, if only informally, that the self-governing dominions, such as South Africa and Australia, might have their own aspirations towards their German colonial neighbours.

The other European powers in Africa had their own views on the subject, but the British made it quite clear, in diplomatic language, that their allies' offers of military assistance in East Africa were unwelcome. The Belgian, Portuguese and even French attempts to contribute contingents against the common enemy were rebuffed early in the war.[22] This may be attributed to British over-confidence in their own abilities to eliminate the Germans as rivals as well as a wish to deny other countries a claim in the potential spoils. Despite the pressing need for military victory over the Central Powers, imperial rivalries and colonial aspirations would remain significant factors throughout the war, and East Africa would be no exception.

However, this littoral strategy did not last very long in its pure form as other factors induced the British to invade German colonies shortly after the outbreak of the war. Sub-imperialism and local fears for security played their part in forming a more aggressive attitude on the part of South Africa and Australia in particular. Both were much more interested in seizing enemy territory than was the British Government and supported active military intervention. Togoland fell by the end of August, while colonial expeditionary forces were being prepared to attack the Cameroons in the north and German South-West Africa in the south.[23] While these campaigns were to drag on much longer than initially expected, it was in East Africa that this alteration to the initial British strategy was to have the most visible effects.

GERMAN POLICY

Germany faced the war in East Africa from two points of view: one from Berlin and the other from Dar-es-Salaam. From the imperial viewpoint, colonies were not a major priority although, prior to the war, efforts had been made to reduce colonial tensions with Britain, actions that had been only partially reciprocated. Indeed, the two powers had initialled the draft of a secret treaty aimed at carving up the Portuguese colonies in the case of an expected financial default.[24] Leaks and unwelcome speculation about the agreement caused the British to lose their nerve for such a deal although the Germans remained keen to press on. However, once hostilities broke out, thoughts of conciliation were quickly forgotten and a more aggressive position was taken. Now at war, the attention of the General Staff and the Government was clearly focused on winning the war in the west before turning east to deal with the Russians. There was virtually no thought given to the fate of the colonies as they were both militarily and economically insignificant.

This is not to say that all interest was lost, as a group in the Government, exemplified by the colonial secretary, Dr Wilhelm Solf, aspired to a German *Mittelafrika*, built on existing colonies and augmented by helpings from the Portuguese- and Belgian-held territories.[25] However, by the end of 1914 all effective links with the colonies had been cut off and, regardless of his aspirations, Solf understood the realities of the strategic situation and that any exchanges of territory would follow a general peace settlement. Furthermore, civilian ministers had been excluded from much of the military planning and decision making, making it difficult to exert any influence on the course of operations.[26]

For the German colonial authorities, the situation was much more pressing as they examined means of surviving the conflict. They realised both the extent of their isolation and the weakness of their own means. In August, the governor initially tried to claim neutrality under the provisions of the Berlin Act 1885, hoping that the other powers would keep Africa out of the war. As Chapter III, Article 10 stated, each of the ruling powers had the option of neutralising their parts of the Congo Basin so long as:

> The Powers which exercise or shall exercise the rights of sovereignty or protectorate over those territories, using their option of proclaiming themselves neutral, shall fulfil the duties which neutrality requires.

Article 11 went on to add that such neutrality required common consent of the powers before becoming effective.[27] Although the telegram of 2 July from the *Reichskolonialamt* (Colonial Office) had raised expectations that such neutrality was being explored, it was punctured several days later by a subsequent report. In the circumstances, there was little enthusiasm by either the British or the Belgians for declaring such neutrality in Africa, especially as the German colonies were so effectively cut off.[28]

This failed attempt to achieve colonial neutrality is an important one as it highlighted one of the fundamental weaknesses of German East Africa's system. This may partially be explained through the German colonial system developing in many different ways than its neighbouring British counterparts. It was marked by the primacy of military over civil aims for much of the early history from its incorporation into the *Reich* in 1892. Like so many colonies, it had been founded through military adventurism and local *faits accomplis*. However, from the outset the military had taken a leading role, with a series of military governors ruling from 1893 to 1905, and civilian voices were often in the minority. Often, the policies of the Imperial Government were quietly ignored, with local commanders claiming a great deal of autonomy even from the governor. Matters changed drastically with the outbreak of the *Maji-Maji* rebellion in 1905 against the harsh policies imposed on the African population. The south-eastern portion of the colony was engulfed by this armed uprising until 1907 as the *Schutztruppe* exacted a bloody vengeance on the rebels and their families. Many villages were razed, headmen hanged and

5. The governor of German East Africa – Dr Heinrich Schnee.

crops left to rot as the military re-asserted its power. At least 75,000 Africans, possibly many more, died, and the area was devastated.[29]

One legacy of *Maji-Maji* had been the formation of a new department, the *Reichskolonialamt*, and the appointment of a series of civilian governors who were charged with the economic development of the protectorates. Critically, the military was placed under the control of the governor so as to reduce their influence and minimise the chances of another large-scale rising. The number of districts under direct military control was reduced from twelve to two out of a total of twenty-two, while less harsh economic and taxation policies were adopted. However, the chronic shortage of civil servants meant that many officers remained involved in administration and others did not accept their subordination with good grace. It must also be said that the process was not uniquely one way, as this was counteracted by the 'civilianisation' of a number of officers employed in adminis- trative work. They gained a personal interest in the development of their districts while losing some of their ardour for the discomforts of military life. Although still retaining their commissions and recalled for active service during the war, a number of the district officers were less than enthusiastic about fighting.

Nevertheless, constant in-fighting and a virulent press campaign forced Governor Rechenberg to resign in 1912 to be replaced by the lawyer and experi- enced colonial official, Dr Heinrich Schnee. Schnee was more sympathetic to the

6. The commander of the *Schutztruppe* – Lt-Col. Paul von Lettow-Vorbeck.

needs of the Africans than the military and made development his main priority. However, he too was to experience this resistance at first hand and such disputes would remain a characteristic feature of his administration.[30]

The tensions between civil policy and the perceived military needs of the districts were to continue, as the duality between the two was partly sustained by Berlin. Although the civilian-run *Reichskolonialamt* oversaw the headquarters of the *Schutztruppe*, its military head was sympathetic to his subordinates' views. For example, as late as the summer of 1914, the headquarters was arguing for the disbandment of the police in militarily occupied territories, a retrograde argument that can have only added to the tension.[31] It is not clear whether Berlin sent out Lettow as a means of continuing this pressure or whether he was simply the most suitable officer. The evidence is intriguing, as he had made a previous request to serve with the colonial forces, but had been rejected by the Colonial Office as being 'unsuitable'. Yet, barely a year later, he was selected to command the force in East Africa then in Cameroon, altered at the last minute back to East Africa. The powerful Military Cabinet had changed the Colonial Office's mind and the new commander (*Kommandeur*) of the *Schutztruppe* arrived in Dar-es-Salaam in January 1914.[32]

The attempt to avoid war was also in accordance with pre-war planning; Berlin had considered this very situation carefully and had correctly concluded that the British were unlikely to accept neutralisation as it went against their direct interests.

Accordingly, they had directed that preparations be made for defending the interior of the colony rather than the coast.[33] This policy had been accepted by both Schnee and Col. von Schleinitz, Lettow's predecessor, and had formed the background for the limited war preparations already made. However, Lettow arrived with completely the opposite opinion and was adamantly opposed to any hint of non-belligerence. He believed that his first duty was to divert as many Allied resources as possible from the main theatre of war. As he said:

> I considered it our military object to detain the enemy, that is English, forces, if it could by any means be accomplished. This however, was impossible if we remained neutral.[34]

Schnee took a much different approach as he wished to preserve the gains made in health, trade and infrastructure since the *Maji-Maji* rebellion. He rightly saw the coming of war as a disaster for his policy of development and did his utmost to prevent it, hoping that his British and Belgian counterparts would think the same way. While many in British East Africa and elsewhere did have similar concerns, governmental pressure from London and Le Havre soon ensured that their colonies were mobilised for operations. With his appeal to the Berlin Act dead, the governor reluctantly began to place German East Africa on a war footing. In the meantime, the military wasted no time and had hurriedly begun the process of mobilising and readying itself for operations, with Lettow ordering companies to increase recruitment and the issuance of arms, munitions and stores from the magazines.[35]

These measures were not universally welcomed as many feared that another large-scale rising would take place on the outbreak of war. There was also a wide-spread feeling that the colonies should be spared from a general war, if only to uphold the prestige of Europeans over their African subjects. These feelings were by no means limited to civilians and were shared by a number of reserve officers who had settled in the colony.[36] However, as time progressed and the threat from the British began to mount perceptibly, attitudes began to change slowly if grudgingly.

Schnee was certainly not the obstinate opponent of military effectiveness that Lettow wished to portray. In many ways, he supported his *Kommandeur* well, as he declared martial law, turned over the bulk of the police force to *Schutztruppe*, and recalled all reservists within days of the declaration to war. However, he refused to hand over all power to the military and retained the right to run the colony, despite Lettow's entreaties to the contrary. For example, Schnee invoked martial law and called up the *Landsturm* on 5 August, retaining executive power to the civil authority, except for cases of urgent danger. Three days later, he turned over the bulk of the police, the posts and telegraphs and railways to military control. Nevertheless, the governor did his best to ensure the security of the colony's borders through neutralisation and, if unsuccessful with the British and Belgians, did achieve it with the Portuguese to the south.[37]

Lettow was a wilful character and was determined to support what he perceived as Germany's greater strategic interests over the concerns of the governor. This was eventually to poison relations between the two men, but in the short term, it was to ensure many bitter and heated arguments about policy.[38] In many cases, the soldier showed himself insubordinate and willing to usurp civil authority as he saw necessary. This lack of unity was to cause confusion and a split in colonial society that would hamper the war effort. However, this conflict was not unique to East Africa, as it mirrored the confused decision-making process of Wilhelmine Germany where the military deliberately excluded civilian ministers from many of its decisions.[39]

THE KING'S AFRICAN RIFLES

In July 1914, the British forces in East Africa were controlled and funded by the Colonial Office. Known as the King's African Rifles (KAR), there were three battalions consisting of some twenty-one infantry companies scattered over an enormous area. Its *raison d'être* was the maintenance of British rule through internal security and frontier defence. Operations were based on the suppression of risings and punishment of marauding tribesmen; participation in a general, modern war had not been seriously considered. It was a typical colonial force of the era in which British officers commanded African non-commissioned officers (NCOs) and men recruited from specific, favoured tribes. The bulk of the troops were actually deployed on operations in the north of British East Africa although the battalions were formally recruited and based as follows: 1 KAR from Nyasaland, 3 KAR from British East Africa and 4 KAR from Uganda.[40]

The total strength of the regiment was nearly 2,400 with sixty-two British officers, two British NCOs and 2,319 Africans.[41] The battalions still followed the old eight single company organisation, which was in the slow process of being phased out, giving each a fighting strength of between seventy-five and 125. Additionally, two of the companies were trained as mounted infantry while a third was camel borne. In peacetime, the inspector-general of the KAR ensured that there was a common administrative and training policy, but isolation and the vast distances involved made detailed control impossible.

Indeed, this situation was quite acceptable to the Colonial Office, as the financially hard-pressed colonies were responsible for paying and equipping the KAR. Apart from seconding officers and supplying arms and equipment, the War Office had little input into the force which lacked a central staff, artillery, medical services and reserves. Nevertheless, the KAR was a well-disciplined and long-service force that was fully acclimatised to fighting in the African bush. It was highly experienced in patrol work and in operating independently in small sub-units. In short, it was an ideal force with which to support any campaign against German East Africa.[42]

7. The King's African Rifles on the march. These experienced troops were turned down by Gen. Aitken.

Alongside the KAR, but under separate civilian control, were the armed colonial police forces of British East Africa and Uganda that numbered fifty Europeans and 1,550 Africans, and twenty-one Europeans and 1,071 Africans, respectively. In many ways a paramilitary force, a considerable number of these police found their way into military service, although initially this was limited by fears of internal unrest and enemy-inspired disorder.[43]

On the outbreak of war, all three battalions were divided between their home territories and Jubaland, near the Somali border, preparing for a punitive expedition against the Turkana. There were no companies near the German border and the Uganda railway was devoid of any protection. Zanzibar and Nairobi each held the equivalent of a company, but the remainder were far to the north. Once hostilities had been declared, the civil authorities lost no time in asking for reinforcements from India as they were concerned about the possibility of risings as well as a direct threat from their German neighbour. In the meantime, the KAR began the lengthy process of redeploying south to face the new threat.[44]

THE *SCHUTZTRUPPE*

Like the KAR, the *Schutztruppe* was little prepared for general war. It too was a force for colonial control and was even more widely scattered in independent company bases. Furthermore, it had a much more serious legacy of unrest and

8. A company of the *Schutztruppe* on a pre-war march.

tribal risings to contend with due to the legacy of the *Maji-Maji* rebellion. Fears of a second rising haunted the minds of many officials and settlers while the memories of the massacres were still very fresh in African minds.

The *Schutztruppe* were roughly equivalent to the KAR in overall numbers, with sixty-three German officers, thirty-two doctors, four officials, sixty-seven NCOs, and 2,542 Africans organised into some fourteen *Feldkompagnien* (*FK*) or field companies. Each *FK* had an establishment of eleven Europeans, 160 Askari, two machine guns and 160 porters; it could carry 17,000 to 18,000 rounds of reserve ammunition plus three days' iron rations. But by mid-September the number of porters was raised to 250 men thereby allowing fourteen days' iron rations and four sets of engineering equipment to be carried.

After the outbreak of hostilities, a number of *Schützenkompagnien* (*Sch K*) were raised throughout the colony. The difference between the *FK* and the *Sch K* was that the former was a drawn largely from the white settler community and shooting clubs. Several were raised from distinct occupations such as the railways and farmers, although there was no set pattern. Apart from carriers, they did not have any Africans and the majority of men had prior military or naval service. Sizes varied with some having as few as forty men and others reaching 120 strong. As they were all Europeans, their personal needs were considered much greater and a very generous establishment of 700 porters was provided.

Weapons were a decidedly limiting factor as the magazines contained only 1,600 old carbines and 579 '1898' pattern rifles of modern design. A much larger number of the old '1871' pattern rifles was available, 10,500 of them, but these had the distinct disadvantage using black powder propellant that emitted a cloud of smoke on firing. The *Sch K* and Germans were issued with the '98 rifle while the bulk of the *FK* had to make do with the much less effective '71 pattern.[45]

The 1911 Instructions for Field Service in German East Africa were very much geared to low-level warfare. They envisaged a mobile company column as having two officers, one doctor, two German NCOs, 150 *Askari*, two machine guns, 322 porters, 100 *Askari* 'boys' and thirteen European 'boys'. Six months' supplies for the Europeans were carried, but only one days' worth for the Africans. Any additional Europeans would be entitled to twenty-two porters each; ten of whom would carry their equipment, tent and cook set, while the remaining six would carry three months' food supplies. The column was rounded off with five riding animals and fifty-four oxen with the whole group capable of moving along the railway in two or three military trains.[46]

This outlook was also reflected in the outlook and mentality of many of the *Schutztruppe*'s officers, few of whom had experience of modern warfare. Independent companies garrisoned the main districts and were protected by prominent high-walled forts, suitably loopholed and occasionally equipped with an antique field piece. On campaign, the standard tactic against a tribal enemy armed with a few muzzleloaders and spears was to adopt an all-round defence, the so-called 'hedgehog'. By tightly bunching together in a square the column was much less easy to outflank, while being able to deliver heavy fire in all directions. This would normally inflict sufficient enemy casualties as to win the day; pursuit was

9. A company of the *Schutztruppe* on a pre-war parade.

10. An *Askari* camp with followers.

often a matter of rounding up the cattle that made up so much of the native Africans' wealth.

However, Lettow had witnessed the effects of magazine-fed rifles and, most especially, machine guns during the Boxer Rebellion and the war in South-West Africa. If such tactics were employed against modern artillery and machine guns, the results would have been devastating for the *Schutztruppe*. His task was not an easy one as the dispersion of the companies and the relative independence of the local commanders made retraining slow. He made a number of changes, with discipline being tightened and an intensive training programme was set in place. He was fortunate too that an old colleague and long-time *Schutztruppe* officer, Tom von Prince, had organised a shooting club for the European reservists, in order to maintain their proficiency.[47]

Lettow was helped in that he had a formidable pool of trained manpower. German East Africa had some 2,700 German and Austro-Hungarian males capable of bearing arms, most of whom belonged to the *Landsturm*. Many had served as either officers or non-commissioned officers before coming out to Africa and understood the need for discipline and training. As well, the navy provided several hundred valuable reinforcements as it placed the crew of the scuttled survey ship *Möwe* and a number of reservists at the *Schutztruppe's* disposal.[48] While there was no formal African reserve, over 600 former *Askari* and 400 *Polizeiaskari* rejoined the colours in 1914. Whatever their immediate limitations, this pool of experienced manpower was to give Lettow a sound base from which to build, although the many new and completely untrained recruits would need a considerable period of training before being ready for the field.[49] By mid-August, the *Schutztruppe* had began the long and deliberate process of leaving their peacetime stations and moving towards concentration areas. War was underway in East Africa.

3

THE DECISION TO DESPATCH INDIAN EXPEDITIONARY FORCES B AND C

In London, with political approval secured, onus now passed to the India Office to execute the plans. The first and least demanding requirement to fulfil was the sending of Indian troops to secure the internal security situation of British East Africa. It was a fairly straightforward task as its mission was the defence of the colony and suppression of any potential African rebellions. The India Office provisionally agreed that three battalions would be sent on 7 August, with the troops making up the force being confirmed ten days later.[1] Brig.-Gen. J.M. Stewart was selected to command the brigade-sized force, now known as Indian Expeditionary Force (IEF) C. Although he and his troops were drawn from the Indian Army, Stewart was placed under the control of the Colonial Office through the governor of British East Africa, Sir H.C. Belfield. With the lead troops already mobilised, Stewart and the 29th Punjabis sailed from Karachi on 19 August, with the rest due to follow as soon as possible thereafter.[2]

However, the fulfilment of the second and more challenging objective, the reduction of Dar-es-Salaam, required more elaborate measures. The India Office had instructed the Viceroy to raise another force, IEF B, on 8 August. This demand for another 8,000 troops in two brigades came at a most unwelcome time to the Army Headquarters as the combined requirements of mobilisation and the sending of the Indian Corps (known as IEF A) to Egypt was placing an immense strain on the existing system. Nevertheless, the next day the Cabinet authorised the despatch of IEF B immediately after IEF A had departed India.[3]

Initially, 16 (Poona) Brigade, under the command of Brig.-Gen. Arthur Aitken, was ordered to form the nucleus of IEF B as troops for the second brigade had not yet been found. On 17 August, Aitken was formally nominated as the overall commander of the expedition and he travelled to Simla ten days later to receive a personal briefing. Neither the Viceroy nor the Commander-in-Chief was enthusiastic about the plan and each had serious reservations about its value, considering

Map 3. The strategic situation in August 1914.

it a dissipation of scarce resources. Regardless of their thoughts, it was the deteriorating relations with the Ottoman Empire that now forced the pace of events. The
British Government considered that reinforcement of the Suez Canal and protection of oil supplies in the Persian Gulf was now paramount and in the circumstances only India could supply the troops. The despatch of IEF B was now
postponed, pending clarification of the situation in the Middle East.[4]

On 28 August, 16 (Poona) Brigade was ordered to Egypt instead of East Africa
although Aitken was to remain in India, keeping his appointment as commander
of IEF B. The news was well received in Army Headquarters, as it was rapidly
running out of troops, while commitments continued to increase. Furthermore,
knowledge of German East Africa and its defenders remained scant. However,
matters soon began to change with the arrival of the former British consul in Dar-
es-Salaam, Mr Norman King, on 25 August. He was an official in the Foreign
Office and a fluent German speaker, and knew all the principal personalities well.
He discussed the situation with the Chief of the General Staff, India before being

appointed the political officer to IEF B on 30 August. Meeting with Aitken the next day, King discussed Aitken's outline plan. It was to land at Dar-es-Salaam, before advancing westward and attacking the Germans entrenched near Pugu, some twelve miles away. Thereafter, he considered that a further, seaborne move on Tanga would effectively end the campaign. King gave Aitken as much information as he could before the latter returned to Poona and King began work on a handbook on German East Africa.[5]

The plan had not been forgotten and was resurrected on 9 September once the immediate crisis in the Persian Gulf had been solved. Helpfully, Army Headquarters had managed to find more troops for the expedition, in the form of a brigade of Imperial Service Troops, drawn from the Princely States' forces while the regular 27 (Bangalore) Brigade was nominated to replace the departed 16 (Poona) Brigade. These were added to the order of battle two days later; IEF B was now up to strength.[6] Subject to final political approval, its start was now dependent on arranging sufficient transport ships and naval escorts.

In the interim, Gen. Barrow was busy in London arranging the command and control arrangements for both IEF B and C. His proposed solution was convoluted and ultimately unworkable, but still met with agreement from the War and Colonial Offices. IEF C was to be placed under the orders of the governor in British East Africa and ultimately the Colonial Office. As its initial role was purely the defence of the colony and similar to that of the KAR, this was viewed as being acceptable and in the normal course of events might have worked. However, offensive operations against German East Africa which would normally have been under the purview of the War Office, because of the strain of war in Europe, were willingly transferred to the India Office. This was not an unprecedented arrangement as India had controlled the operations in China during the Boxer Rebellion of 1900. In this case, Aitken would receive his general instructions from the Secretary of State for India, having consulted with the Colonial Office and the Admiralty.

However, problems arose when the two forces came together. In British East Africa IEF B would be under India's control, while for defensive matters IEF C would work to the Colonial Office. But, it had been agreed that some troops from the latter force would assist IEF B in its offensive operations against German East Africa, while the remainder continued to guard British territory. The upshot of this arrangement was that IEF B and those others who proceeded into German territory would come under Aitken's command and hence India, but the rest would stay under Colonial Office control. Finally, if things were not complex enough, the Admiralty, through the local commander-in-chief, would provide support for the expedition, although Aitken would have no authority over the ships.

While preserving the authority of each department, such distinctions were militarily unworkable and bound to break down under the pressure of war. The Colonial Office contended that it should retain control of operations regardless of the presence of a senior force commander. Despite not having any direct colonial experience or indeed any military officers on its staff, it considered itself the sole authority on colonial defence, 'any difference of opinion on that point being referred to the Colonial Office, who are alone responsible for their internal security.'[7]

The weakness of this attitude was exposed almost immediately after the arrival of IEF C when, as instructed by India, Gen. Stewart signalled his plans to the War Office and Army Headquarters. He was firmly and immediately rebuked by the Colonial Secretary, being forbidden to make direct communications with either department and told that any requests should go through his office. Harcourt stated 'The troops of Expedition C were therefore under the control of the Governor who should refer, if necessary, to the S. of S. for the Colonies.'[8]

While this complied with existing departmental practices, it ignored the vital factors that British and Indian reinforcements were not under the Colonial Office's authority, while technical stores, weapons, ammunition and equipment were controlled by either the War Office or Army Headquarters. Putting aside questions of policy, the denial of routine communication was bound to create unnecessary delay and confusion. If these methods had worked in the past when dealing with low-level tribal insurrections, they were doomed to confusion when faced with a modern and well-trained enemy such as the Germans.

Having confirmed the byzantine command arrangements, Barrow then produced a revised instruction for the general officer commanding (GOC) that far exceeded the earlier intentions. Instead of the initial modest aims of destroying a wireless station and occupying the only major port facilities held by the Germans in the Indian Ocean:

> The object of the expedition under your command is to bring the whole of German East Africa under British authority... you should, in the first instance, secure the safety of British East Africa by occupying the north-eastern portion of the German Colony viz., the country between Tanga and Kilimanjaro. For this purpose, it is suggested that you should first occupy Tanga with Expedition 'B', and that, when this movement has had its due moral effect on the Germans in hinterland of Tanga, Expedition 'C' should, if feasible, advance from Tsavo and threaten Moshi. It is, however, for you to judge whether such an operation is practicable and advisable, also whether Expedition 'C' should be strengthened by you for this object.[9]

Having taken Tanga, he was also instructed to consider an assault on Dar-es-Salaam as a subsequent task. IEF B, which numbered just short of 8,000 soldiers, and assisted by IEF C, of about 2,000 Indians and Africans, was to capture a vast and wild area, some one and a half times the size of Imperial Germany.[10] In the circumstances, Barrow's grandiose plans may have looked plausible. But there is no evidence that he produced a reasoned appreciation of the situation based on the realities of either the military force available or the conditions in German East Africa. He seems simply to have decided that the capture of the entire colony was a good idea and that the two brigades earmarked for it were adequate.

THE RAISING OF IEF B

The sending of the expedition against German East Africa was destined to wait as higher priority forces were despatched. The sending of the Indian Corps in IEF A was to absorb most of the available shipping and convoy resources from late August to the middle of September. Then, apart from the staggered move of IEF C to Mombasa, the Admiralty had to make provisions for the initial movement of IEF D to the Persian Gulf that coincided with the departure of Aitken's force. Finally, the depredations of the *Emden* would delay the concentration of ships from Calcutta to Bombay – it would be impossible to sail before 16 October. The *Königsberg* remained a considerable worry as Churchill ordered that all convoys must have at least two warships in escort, one of which had to be stronger than the German ship. This of course delayed matters and slowed down the shipment of troops and materials.[11]

Equally important to the successful execution of the plan to conquer the German colony was the character and experience of the commander, Gen. Arthur Aitken. Aged fifty-three years in 1914, he was an infantry officer who was initially commissioned into the Worcestershire Regiment before transferring to the Indian Army in 1882. He had risen to battalion command of the 119th Infantry in 1904, and after seven years there, he took over 16 (Poona) Brigade in 1911. As such, he was a highly experienced officer with nearly three years spent as a brigadier general. Compared to contemporaries, his active service had been limited, taking part only in the Sudan campaign of 1885 as a young officer. His abilities had not attracted a great deal of attention and he was not well known within the army. Subordinates noted that he had a pompous manner and seemed to be dominated by his chief of staff. He was easy to work with, but did not give the impression of intellect or being a student of war. Some believed him to be a 'dud' and others had little real confidence in their commander. It is apparent that the best officers were keen to go with IEF A and that East Africa was an unpopular sideshow, so much so that his force was nicknamed 'Aitken's Menagerie'.[13] However, with a bristling grey moustache, tanned face and portly build, he had the looks and manner of a confident general even if he was far from the forefront of Indian Army officers.[14]

His brigadiers were of a decidedly mixed background. The first, Brig.-Gen. Richard Wapshare, was a cavalry officer who was a close contemporary of Aitken's. He had actually started his career in the Royal Marines before joining the Indian Army in 1882. He became a cavalry officer and commanded the 30th Lancers between 1903 and 1910. The following two years were spent as commandant of the new cavalry school at Saugor before taking command of 27 (Bangalore) Brigade in 1912. Despite his background, this was a predominantly infantry formation, although it also had two cavalry regiments attached. He had seen active service in Burma during the 1886–88 campaign, but had not come to any distinction. He appears as a rather conventional and decent officer who was devoted to his family and whose rise had been through seniority and application rather than outstanding talent. Wapshare was rather stout as he took little exercise and enjoyed the comforts of life fully. While liked, he did not inspire great confidence in his subordinates who considered him nervous and fussy. He was not an energetic commander and lacked a sense of dynamism and drive. Like Aitken, he does not appear to have studied his profession nor to have been particularly up to date in military developments.[15]

By contrast, the commander of the Imperial Service Brigade, Brig.–Gen. Michael Tighe was a well-respected officer with a long record of active service. Fifty years old, he was four years younger than Aitken, but had considerably more fighting experience. He was an Irishman who had been commissioned in the Leinster Regiment before switching to the Indian Army in 1885. He had fought alongside Wapshare in the Burma campaign of 1886–88, followed by the Karen Field Force in 1888–89. He had done well serving in the mounted infantry, gaining the Distinguished Service Order and a mention in Despatches. After a further period on the north-east frontier, Tighe was sent to East Africa in 1896 and Uganda in 1898–99 to suppress a mutiny. He received another mention in Despatches and was promoted brevet major. Finally, he commanded the Mekran frontier expedition in 1901 where he received another mention and a brevet lieutenant-colonelcy.

Tighe went on to command the 56th Punjabi Rifles, a frontier force unit, before retiring to England as a colonel in August 1913. On the outbreak of war, he returned immediately to India and was promoted brigadier general in September 1914. He was given command of the newly created Imperial Service Brigade in the same month. Unlike Aitken and Wapshare, Tighe was renowned for his courageousness and desire to be in the thick of any fight. He had an attractive and outgoing personality that appealed to soldiers. However, brave and dynamic as he was, he was not thought to be particularly thoughtful or reflective – he was a fighting officer who had made his name dealing with fierce and lightly armed tribesmen on the fringes of empire. Importantly, though, he had served in East Africa and knew the problems that bush warfare presented.[16]

The selection of IEF B was far from smooth as the changes in plan and the inexorable rise in commitments disrupted mobilisation. In 27 (Bangalore) Brigade, the cavalry and artillery units were detached to other formations, while half of its integral infantry battalions were changed. The 61st Pioneers were detached as divisional troops and the 108th Infantry was sent elsewhere; they were replaced by 63rd Palamcottah Light Infantry from Kamptree in the north and the 98th Infantry from Saugor in central India. This left only two of the original four units, the 2nd Loyal North Lancashires and 101st Grenadiers, in Bangalore.

Mobilisation of the brigade was slow, and by 22 September the 61st Pioneers were still not ready for active service. This was only completed in October, with the battalion reaching Bombay on 7 October and embarking the next afternoon.[17] Matters were much worse in the north as the 63rd Palamcottah Light Infantry

11. Brigadier generals Michael Tighe (l) and Richard Wapshare (r).

boarded ship in Karachi on 30 September, remaining on board for the sixteen days before sailing, while the mountain battery, the sappers and miners joined them later. Indeed, Gen. Wapshare never saw his entire brigade on land before departing for operations.

For the Imperial Service Brigade matters were worse as it was an entirely new force. Gen. Tighe was faced with bringing together a scratch formation that, apart from the 13th Rajputs, was based on non-Indian Army troops, the so-called Imperial Service Corps. These troops were regular soldiers who were raised, trained and paid for by the Princely States and were substantially less well equipped than their Indian Army counterparts. The Imperial Service troops were of a highly variable standard although the Kashmir forces had the advantage of constant active service on the frontier. Unusually for the period, they were commanded by Indian officers although one or two British officers were attached to ensure standardisation and reliability. Whatever their background, Imperial Service units were not considered to be crack units.

Tighe was allocated the equivalent of three battalions; a half battalion each of 2nd Kashmir Rifles and 3rd Gwalior Rifles to operate together, the 3rd Battalion Kashmir Rifles and the regular 13th Rajputs. Apart from the Kashmiris, none had worked together previously and the brigade was only brought together some six

12. The officers of the 2nd Battalion, Loyal North Lancashire Regiment in Bangalore, September 1914.

days before sailing. As an example of the difficulties, the 13th Rajputs had been warned of their mobilisation with Force 'B' on 11 September, but spent the next two weeks split up on railway defences where a number of men contracted malaria. The battalion joined its fellows at Deolali on 1 October where it spent four days training. The battalion then left for Bombay on 6 October, which it reached a day later, before embarking on 8 October.[18] If time had been extremely short, at least Tighe had concentrated his troops and conducted some preliminary training before departure. This was considerably more than Wapshare achieved.

If the process of bringing the force together was fraught with difficulty, then completing mobilisation was even worse. The first was organisational as infantry battalions had been in the process of changing from the existing eight (single) companies, each commanded by a captain to one of four (double) companies led by majors. This process was by no means complete and the new structure was still unfamiliar to many. Weaponry was the second, as on the outbreak of war, units in southern India had not yet received the new short magazine Lee-Enfield rifle (SMLE) and still retained the obsolete longer version. These had to be issued hastily just prior to embarkation, but many soldiers were not fully proficient in its use or the rifle's sighting system. The situation was worse with the Kashmiris who still retained the even older Martini-Henry rifles and had to adapt to the new weapon very rapidly.[19]

Finally, only the 2nd North Lancashire, the 61st Pioneers and the 101st Grenadiers had been issued with machine guns during peacetime. All the remaining units had to improvise detachments and conduct hurried training on this important weapons system. The unfortunate 63rd Light Infantry only took charge of theirs whilst on board ship. In the Imperial Service Brigade the situation was even worse; only the 13th Rajputs had machine guns with none of the other battalions being given any at all. Manpower was another important deficiency as many units had to be brought up to strength. Both the 61st Pioneers and 63rd Light Infantry had to be reinforced by large drafts from linked battalions, while in the 13th Rajputs nearly half the British officers came from other units.[20]

Finally, by mid-October, all the units were loaded and the ships ready to depart for East Africa. Now departure depended on the naval situation which was becoming more favourable to the British. Spee's East Asiatic Squadron had been located in Pacific waters while the *Königsberg* was reckoned to be hiding along the East African coast. However, in September, the balance of forces was changed with the sudden appearance of SMS *Emden* in the Bay of Bengal. This caused considerable alarm, but unless the two enemy cruisers could link up, the escorting guns of HMS *Goliath*, an elderly battleship, and the *Fox*, a light cruiser, were deemed sufficient to protect IEF B. By 16 October, the orders to sail were given and two great convoys left Bombay and Karachi heading west. The fight for German East Africa was about to begin.[21]

The commander of IEF B briefed his officers at a conference in Bombay just prior to departure. There, he stated that he intended to land at either port, depending on the situation along the Anglo-German border on arrival at Mombasa. Making light of the importance of the task given to him, he promised

13. The British officers of the 98th Infantry on board the SS *Nairung*.

14 & 15. The 98th Infantry loading at Bombay.

to send all the best officers to France as soon as it was completed. Finally, he summed up with a statement of his concerns:

> There is one thing, gentlemen, about which I feel very strongly… that is the subject of dress. I wish officers and men to be always well turned out... I will not tolerate the appalling sloppiness allowed during the Boer War.[12]

With such inspiring and thought-provoking remarks IEF B prepared to go to war.

The Despatch of IEF C

IEF C had been authorised by the Cabinet on 6 August, but it would be several weeks before the troops were ready to depart. Even then, there was insufficient shipping to carry the entire contingent, and only Force Headquarters, the 29th Punjabis and a medical detachment departed from Karachi on the troopship *Nairung* on 19 August. The journey was uneventful and escorted by two warships, the Indians arrived safely in Mombasa eight days later. The Punjabis were immediately split in half, with one group going to the Voi-Tsavo area opposite Kilimanjaro and the remainder to Nairobi. There, Brig.-Gen. Stewart established his headquarters.[22]

16. An Ahir company of the 98th Infantry.

17. Troops of the 29th Punjabis.

In the meantime, British efforts were directed at recalling the bulk of the KAR from Jubaland and organising their defences particularly along the vulnerable Uganda Railway and the Kilimanjaro area. Effort was expended re-enlisting former soldiers and finding recruits to make up under-strength companies, while over 1,800 Europeans volunteered for service in a number of extemporised units. However, it would take some considerable time before such troops would be ready for serious military operations against a trained enemy.

The first incursion into British territory came on 14/15 August when the Germans occupied the border post of Taveta several miles inside the frontier. As this place was the last significant water hole for many miles, the defenders retreated back towards Voi leaving an arid no-man's land between them and the Germans. Further concerns about the security of the colony came in late August, when the Giriama tribe attacked several European civil posts. This required the diversion of a number of KAR troops, first to subdue the warriors and then to patrol the area to prevent a recurrence. While successfully put down this was precisely the type of problem that colonial administrators feared, and it drained military resources.[23]

By early September, the troops available in British East Africa numbered about 3,400, being spread from a detachment on Lake Victoria to about 1,100 in Nairobi to a similar number around Voi and about 400 on the coast. Distant Uganda contained just under 1,000, but many of these were far from being fully trained.[24]

The situation was remedied somewhat by the arrival of the remainder of IEF C in late September. This comprised four half battalions of Imperial Service infantry provided by the states of Bharatpur, Jind, Kapurthala and Rampur together with the 27th Mountain Battery, the Calcutta Volunteer Battery and the Railway Machine Gun Volunteers. It was a decidedly mixed force with only limited offensive capability. However, it brought firepower and numbers to the thinly stretched KAR garrison.[25]

GERMAN REACTIONS

Command of the *Schutztruppe* lay with Col. Lettow, a man very different from his British contemporaries. He came from a noble Pomeranian family with a long tradition of military service. Aged forty-four years in 1914, Lettow was a highly professional and well-educated man, speaking both French and English. He was well connected, both militarily and socially, and began his army career as a subaltern in the *4. Garderegiment zu Fuß*. He was a hard-working and ambitious officer who passed into the Great General Staff in 1899. He served on the staff during the Boxer Rebellion of 1900–01 where he had opportunity to work with various foreign armies, including the British forces. Subsequently, he participated in the suppression of the Herero revolt in German South-West Africa, firstly on von Trotha's staff and latterly as a company commander.

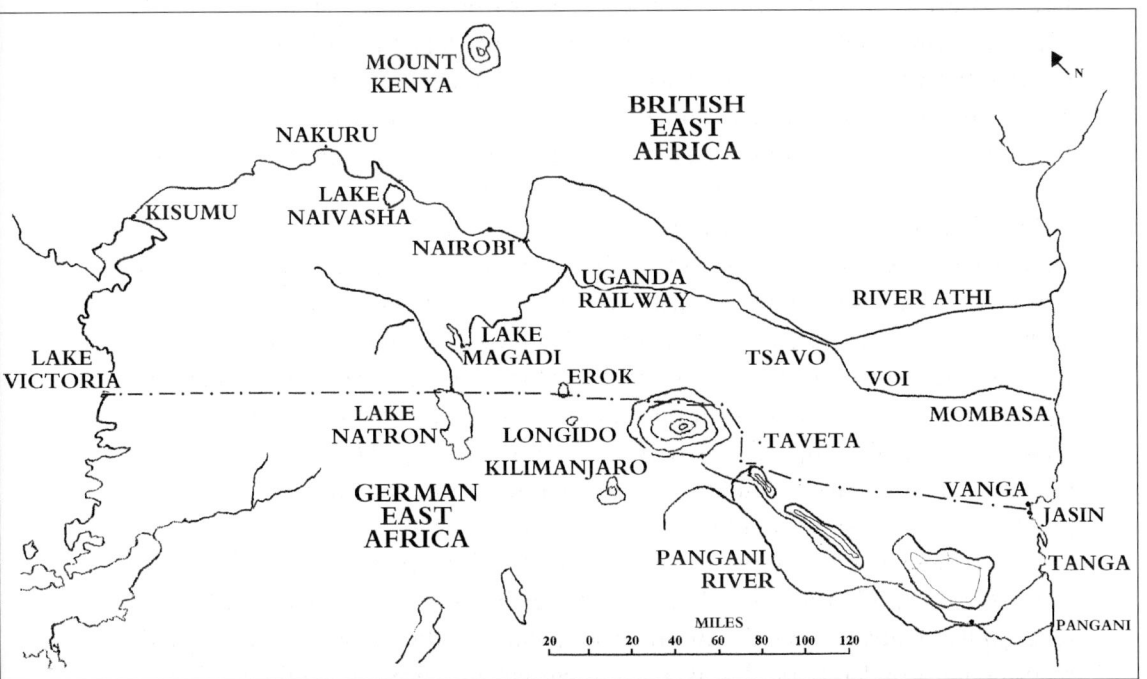

Map 4. The northern area.

18. German headquarters on the coast.

19. German soldiers on the coast.

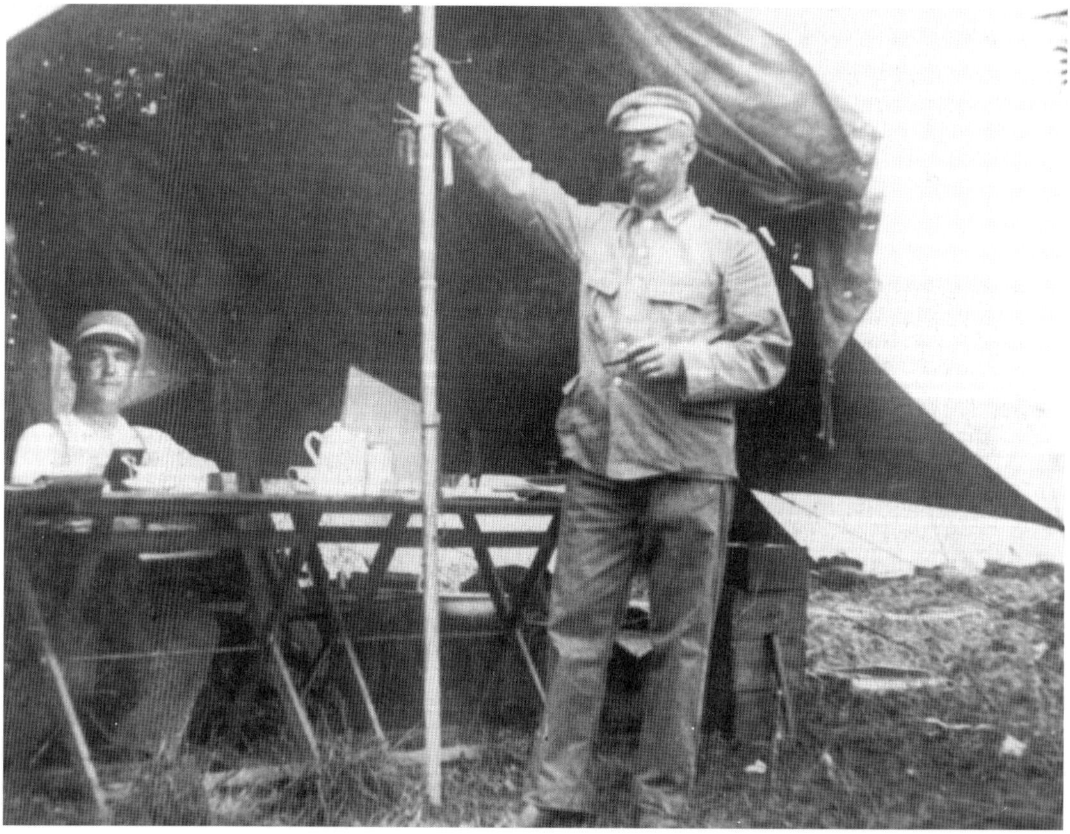

On return to Germany, Lettow took up another General Staff appointment, this time as adjutant to XI Corps in Kassel. After three years there, he was posted to Wilhelmshafen, where he assumed command of *2. Seebatallion* until 1913. Finally, he was selected to command the *Schutztruppe* in German East Africa only to be informed a few months later that he was going to Cameroon instead. This was changed back to East Africa at the end of 1913 and Lettow departed soon afterward, arriving in Dar-es-Salaam at the beginning of 1914.[26]

Lettow was a man of determination and drive. He had had a highly successful career and had gained a great deal of experience of warfare under difficult conditions. He could be polite and well mannered, but equally could be stubborn and ruthless. He had very firm views on military strategy and would not hesitate to act without higher authority. Above all, he was determined to divert as many British resources to East Africa as possible, regardless of the governor's concerns.

With the distances and the dispersed nature of their forces, the initial German concentration took the better part of August and major deployments to the forward areas began in early September. By 8 September, Lettow had collected some eleven companies in and around Kilimanjaro with one protecting the Usambara railway and another guarding Neu Moschi itself. Three companies remained to secure the Central Railway.[27] Two battalions were formed each of four companies: *I Batallion* (Maj. Kepler) was based near Himo while the *II Batallion* (Capt. Baumstark), was sent off to the coast to deal with the potential threats there. It had been the discovery that the British were collecting large numbers of porters, some 2,000 at Voi and 3,000 at Mombasa, that led to this reshuffling of forces.

20. A *Feldkompagnie* in camp.

21. German *Askaris* cleaning rifles.

They were faced by far-from-overwhelming numbers, as the British had about 3,400 soldiers scattered from Lake Victoria to Mombasa with a further 1,000 in Uganda. About 1,100 were in the Voi-Tsavo area with another 1,100 at Nairobi and 300 on the coast. The lead battalion of IEF C, the 29th Punjabis, numbering over 700, had only just arrived and the remainder of that force, some 2,000 additional men, was still concentrated in India.[28]

Baumstark had been ordered to move on the British positions at Vanga and Gazi and then to destroy the Uganda Railway. An attack on 22 September on Majoreni convinced the British that the *II Batallion* and the *Königsberg* might launch a concerted assault on Mombasa and three days later, the post was abandoned while reinforcements were hurriedly sent to Gazi. However, Baumstark's lethargic pursuit enabled the British to regroup and the newly arrived second wave of IEF C was added to the troops holding the coast.[29] This changed the situation as the 500 Germans now faced over 800 British troops. After a fruitless attack on 7 October, Baumstark fell back on Jasin, leaving his opponents on the field of battle.[30]

On 1 November, the *Schutztruppe* was deployed with the bulk of its northern forces, some fourteen out of twenty companies, in the Kilimanjaro area. Divided into four *Abteilungen*, *Abt von Prince* (three companies) in Taveta; *Abt Kepler* (four companies) at Tsavo; *Abt Kraut* (four companies) holding Longido; and Headquarters (three companies) in reserve at Neu Moschi. A further two weak companies were engaged on railway defence duties with the remaining four of *II Batallion* under Baumstark in the coastal area.[31]

4

LOCAL NAVAL OPERATIONS
AND THE ILL-FATED TRUCE

In 1914, Tanga was the second port in German East Africa after Dar-es-Salaam. It is sited on the coast about 140 miles north of the capital and some forty miles south of the British border post at Vanga. It lies upon the narrow coastal plain that begins around Mombasa and then carries on to Dar-es-Salaam, widening as it approaches the basins of the mighty Rufiji and Rovuma Rivers. The land itself is hot, low-lying, humid and covered with thick vegetation. The area is well watered by the annual monsoon rains with two distinct rainy seasons, the 'short rains' of October–November and the 'long rains' of January–April. It is home to a number of indigenous tropical diseases, with the anopheles mosquito-borne malaria presenting one of the biggest hazards to health, particularly during the wet seasons.

On the seafront, Tanga lay about 10ft above sea level with sandy beaches sweeping to either side. The town itself was laid out in a geometrical pattern with separate quarters for the European and African populations with heavy vegetation abounding on the fringes. There were about 900 houses, of which eighty of the most important were built of stone and concentrated near the harbour. One major street ran parallel to the harbour's edge with most of the important governmental and commercial buildings laying along it. Fundamental to Tanga's status as a trade centre was the presence of the eastern terminus of the Usambara railway. This single track line ran all the way from the fertile and well-populated Kilimanjaro district in the north, then along the heavily wooded Pangani Valley, finally sweeping towards Tanga and the sea. The line bisected the European and African quarters, with the main station in the centre of the town, before turning north and running through a deep cutting and emerging onto the jetty.

To the north and west of Tanga, there were a number of large European planta-tions at Amboni, Kiomani, Mayonyo, Pongwe and Kange with the latter two having small railway stations. The eastern limit of the town was marked by the railway cutting, which was crossed by three small bridges. Moving east toward the coast, there was a belt of cultivated ground covered in large numbers of mango and coconut. There was a great deal of tall grass throughout this area together with a

22. A view of Tanga from the west.

number of scattered African huts and dwellings. A shallow drainage ditch that paralleled the railway cutting, running roughly north–south, was a prominent feature as was the European cemetery further east. North of this and along the waterfront were the imposing stone buildings of the government hospital set in its own grounds.

After about 400 yards, the ground cover changed to the rubber and sisal crops of the Möhn Plantation that extended almost to the coastal cliffs. In the north the bush was extremely thick and difficult to penetrate whereas further south the rubber plantations consisted of well-spaced trees and relatively little undergrowth. Movement was by two parallel roads which ran from Tanga towards the coast, with the northerly one known as the 'Hospital Road' and the southerly called the 'Askari Road'. There were also a number of well-defined tracks throughout the area. The Tanga peninsula swept north to the promontory of Ras Kasone with its distinctive signal tower, before moving south towards Pangani. The eastern limits of the land feature ended as well-defined cliffs, about 20–30ft high, that overlooked narrow muddy beaches that were home to large numbers of mangrove trees.

As a port, Tanga was not well developed in either size or capacity having only a single jetty and no cranes. The bay was quite large and was divided into two parts, the smaller inner harbour in the south, and the larger outer harbour that extended from the promontory at Ras Kasone in the south to Ulenge Island in the north. The town and jetty could only be approached through the narrow channel formed between Ras Kasone and Toten Island in the inner harbour. With the four fathom (24ft) line well away from shore, the water was too shallow to permit large ships to tie up on the pier and it was necessary to tranship loads via tugs and lighters. The outer harbour was much deeper, but it was fringed by a number of coral reefs and more exposed to the surf. In the northern part of the bay, the broad entrance of the River Sigi appeared usable, but was in fact too shallow for navigation. About 500 yards offshore, a large coral reef presented a significant obstacle to ships, although boats could cross it at high water.[1]

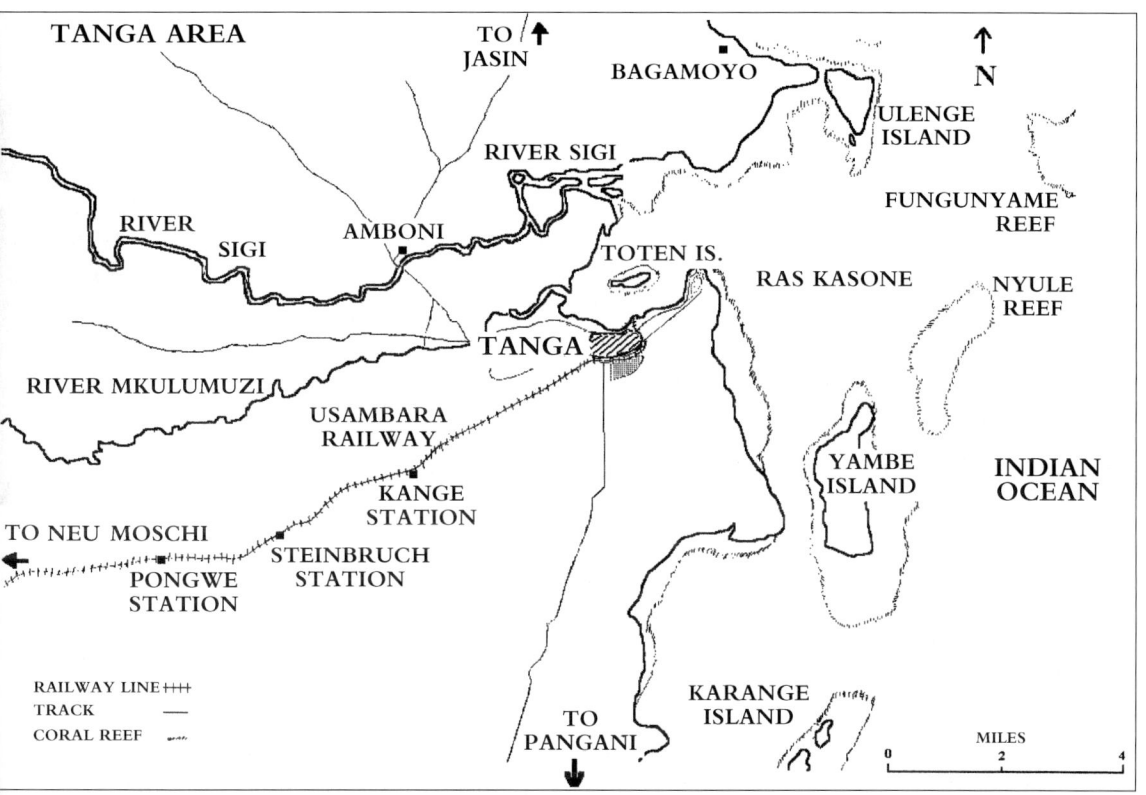

Map 5. Tanga area.

By late October, the German forces were largely concentrated in the area around Mount Kilimanjaro, occupying both the best farming country and the optimal land approach to British East Africa. In order to sustain these large forces in such a small area, they had established a long and difficult line of communication from the western railhead at Neu Moschi to Mombo and thence to Tanga. With the Royal Navy's constant patrolling of the coastal waters, Lettow had established a small trolley line south from Mombo to Handeni and thence overland to the Central Railway. The middle portion was the slowest and least efficient of the journey and it was essential to move supplies as quickly as possible up through the Pangani Valley as it was infested with malarial mosquitoes and tsetse fly. The Usambara Railway was critical to the maintenance of the Kilimanjaro position and Tanga was its main maintenance centre.

The *Schutztruppe* had also established a significant detachment on the coast road leading to the British post of Vanga. The intention was to prevent any move south from Mombasa towards Tanga as well as to launch raids on the British railway system. Tanga was the main base for this force, and its loss would make its position untenable.

Equally important, the town was weakly defended, having only one platoon of 17 FK in the town itself, with two others stationed several miles to the west. This company was a recent addition to the defence force, having previously been employed as armed police which had been placed on military service on the

23. The African quarter, Tanga.

24. The European hospital, Tanga.

outbreak of war.[2] The problems of civil-military relations have already been noted as has the standing plan to leave the coastal towns undefended and to hold the interior. It was to be Schnee's desire to continue his policy of minimal belligerence as well as British concern to neutralise the *Königsberg* that led to several local truces being agreed shortly after the outbreak of war.

These truces, which symptomised much of what went wrong at Tanga and the early stages of the East African campaign, require some explanation. It began with the enterprising action of several ships' captains who sought to render the German coastal ports ineffective as bases for the *Königsberg*. In August 1914, HMS *Astraea* was ordered to neutralise the long-range wireless station at Dar-es-Salaam. After a short bombardment on 8 August, the German authorities raised the white flag and were presented with an ultimatum. Essentially, they were given the choice between further bombardment or establishing a truce, in which all warlike materials were to be removed and all hostile activity was to be renounced for the duration of the war.[3] In return, the British would leave the towns undisturbed. This action was repeated a few days later (17 August) at Tanga with similar terms.[4] While seemingly severe, these conditions actually met with Governor Schnee's approbation as they offered security to the colony's most vulnerable points and coincided with the pre-war plans to defend the interior. The truces seemed an ideal way of limiting the effects of the war while maintaining territorial integrity. On the British side, at least locally, the agreements appeared to reduce the *Königsberg*'s options considerably and permitted their warships to remove anything of military value.

Critically, the ships' captains stipulated that ratification of the agreements was subject to the approval of the British Government which would be sought via the Admiralty; for their part, the German civil authorities were only too happy to consider the truce as immediately binding without further need for approval. However, the military commander was violently opposed to any such accommo-

25. HMS *Astraea* off the East African coast.

26. Usambara Street, Tanga.

27. The old *Boma*, Tanga – formerly for defence and now used for officials' quarters.

dation and had a number of stormy discussions with the governor on the subject. Overruled in the short term, Lettow would not let the subject drop in the coming months, believing that it undermined his aggressive strategy.

With the coast apparently neutralised and the German cruiser having disappeared, two of the ships were ordered back to South Africa to assist in convoy escorts and the planned landings in German South-West Africa, leaving only the slow and outgunned *Pegasus* behind. Concerns about its being unable to deal with the *Königsberg* were dismissed as being a 'slight risk' and the security of the East Coast was left to an obsolete cruiser and a number of small craft.[5]

On 26 August, less than a fortnight after the imposition of the Tanga truce, the Admiralty signalled the Commander-in-Chief, Cape of Good Hope Station, refusing to ratify the terms. It was realised that local, other than temporary, truces were incompatible with general war and that they could inhibit British freedom of action, especially as the landings at Dar-es-Salaam were still being contemplated.[6] In fact, an order limiting local truces was subsequently issued to the fleet in light of the East African experience. However, in a rather devious move, the Admiralty deferred making a decision as to whether an immediate disclaimer to the Germans was necessary, leaving the decision to Admiral King-Hall. Happy to continue the subterfuge, he thought it unnecessary, as an early repudiation would allow the Germans to prepare defences.[7] Accordingly, the Senior Naval Officer (SNO) Mombasa was informed by signal on 30 August that:

> H.M.G. does not ratify terms of truce Dar-es-Salaam and Tanga. You should inform Governors of the two towns of this at a convenient opportunity shortly before any further offensive action is taken against either of the towns.[8]

This decision was taken in full knowledge of the planned landings in East Africa, as the Admiralty had been closely involved in the planning and preparations of IEF B's deployment. While it was confident that sufficient time was available to repudiate the truces before the start of active operations, other ministries were not. The Colonial Secretary, Lewis Harcourt, was concerned enough to ask for written assurances;[9] these were given on 26 August with the Foreign Office, India Office and War Office included in the correspondence.[10] The matter appears to have been given little further thought, as it seems likely that all presumed that these instructions would be interpreted in an intelligent and timely fashion. Knowing that it would be some time before IEF B arrived off the east coast of Africa, the advice of the Commander-in-Chief Cape was accepted and the unratified truces were allowed to stand for the time being.

> No immediate disclaimer considered necessary unless immediate action against them is contemplated when it would be advisable to inform them of expiration of truce at a certain date otherwise defences might be prepared and advantage of having imposed truce will be lost.

28. Rear Admiral Herbert King-Hall (r) and his brother, Admiral Sir George King-Hall (l).

The Admiralty agreed with King-Hall's telegram, noting:

> Concur. The expedition against German East Africa is not likely to commence for some weeks. Action can be taken before it leaves Zanzibar.[11]

The dangers to IEF B were highlighted by the surprise re-appearance of the *Königsberg* in East African waters in late September. In defiance of instructions, the *Pegasus* was caught making repairs in Zanzibar harbour with all steam off and unable to move. Early on 20 September, the ship was overwhelmed and sunk with heavy loss by a surprise attack by the German cruiser. This substantially altered the situation in British eyes, as it removed the only cruiser on the East African coast while the Cape Squadron was totally overstretched as it had to support the planned landings in German South-West Africa with its two remaining ships. At the same time, convoys from India and the Pacific had to continue unimpeded despite the threat posed by the *Emden*. The immediate response was the sending of three fast cruisers from Aden to hunt the *Königsberg* while the *Fox* remained on station after having brought IEF C safely to Mombasa.[12] On 1 October, with the forthcoming expedition against German East Africa in mind, control of East African waters north of Delagoa Bay was transferred to the Commander-in-Chief, East Indies.[13] The naval situation was now firmly tilted in British favour.

Since the beginning of the month, the British cruisers were scouring the East African coast for signs of the elusive *Königsberg*. However, information was beginning to filter through to the British. In mid-month they learned that the ocean-going tug *Adjutant* was sailing from the neutral Portuguese port of Beira to

Lindi where a steamer named *Präsident* was moored. Suspecting that the tug was actually in support of the light cruiser, the *Chatham* sailed into Lindi harbour on 19 October under a flag of truce. The *Bezirkamtsmann* assured the British that the *Präsident* was a hospital ship, but as it was incorrectly marked and appeared on no register, the landing party decided to investigate further. Apart from a lack of medical activity, it found some far more interesting information on the bridge: a receipt for coal sent to Salale and charts of the Rufiji mouth. With these vital hints, the navy went off to find its dangerous quarry.[14]

Intelligence reports and the fate of the *Pegasus* convinced the British, incorrectly as it transpired, that the *Königsberg* had been surreptitiously visiting the truce-bound ports. This led to the cruiser *Chatham* steaming to Dar-es-Salaam on 21 October in search of the warship. Seeing what appeared to be a functioning wireless mast in the harbour, the ship opened fire, only stopping when the Germans hurriedly raised a white flag.[15] Returning the next day, a landing party that included the Army's chief intelligence officer, Lt-Col. Mackay, and the former British consul examined the harbour and took photographs of the site. There was no sign of the *Königsberg* or indeed of any warlike preparations while the only casualties were a number of Indian stokers who were British subjects.[16] They spoke to the civil representatives who complained rightly that the shelling had broken the truce. To resolve matters, the Germans were taken on board the *Chatham* and met Capt. S.R. Drury-Lowe who told them that the sinking of the *Pegasus* had rendered the agreement null and void. Furthermore, he considered that his squadron knew nothing of such agreements and that it was 'invalid'.[17] The Germans were now under no illusions about the validity of the truce and nor should the Admiralty or the respective commanders-in-chief be as Drury-Lowe signalled them the following day:

Informed Acting Governor I considered truce arranged by ASTRAEA & PEGASUS with Dar es Salaam & Tanga was to be disregarded after sinking

29. SMS *Königsberg* entering the Rufiji Delta.

of PEGASUS by KONIGSBERG & also as many reports received KONIGSBERG had been using harbour.[18]

There was no question that the SNO, Capt. F.W. Caulfeild, on HMS *Fox*, was aware of the situation as King, now back in East Africa, fully updated the naval officer on 26 October. It was evident that the situation was becoming hopelessly muddled as the truces had been rejected by the British Government. But, the navy observed them in a haphazard manner and after the loss of the *Pegasus*, considered them invalid – apart from the SNO, it seems. For the German part, the civil authorities, backed by the governor, still supported the truces, but were thwarted whenever possible by Lettow and his military subordinates. It was a recipe for disaster.

Despite Drury-Lowe's actions, Caulfeild still was under the opinion that the Germans ought to be notified that the truces were cancelled.[19] However, he does not appear to have sought the opinion of his commander-in-chief on this important issue. Caulfeild knew that IEF B was *en route* and that a landing in East Africa was expected at either Dar-es-Salaam or Tanga. He may have been influenced by a written note from the Commander-in-Chief, Cape Squadron, to the Resident at Zanzibar that notification of the non-ratification of the truces should be conveyed to the respective governors shortly before any hostile act.[20] However, command of the area had passed to the East Indies station over three weeks previously and the situation had changed radically with the loss of the *Pegasus*. It would have been prudent to clarify such an important matter while time remained.

In the meantime, the bulk of IEF B had left Bombay on 16 October while the remainder departed from Karachi the same day, all as part of the great imperial convoy sailing west. Meeting up on 19 October, the twelve troopships bound for East Africa were led south by HMS *Goliath* and RIMS *Hardinge*, an armed transport vessel.[21] Progress was slow and uneventful with very hot weather encountered as it crossed the equator. The convoy arrived off Mombasa on 30 October, meeting up with the *Fox* for the first time and a conference ensued on board SS *Karmala*, carrying the force headquarters. The SNO, acting on his commander-in-chief's instructions, tried to induce Aitken to travel on his ship in the interests of co-ordination. This he was unable to do and the general remained on his troopship with his staff.[22] However, during the meeting a number of important pieces of intelligence were passed to Aitken and his staff, including for the first time the news of the naval truces. The force intelligence officer noted:

> Detail of the Terms of Truce arranged between His Majesty's Navy at DARESALAM & TANGA & subsequent action of H.M.S. 'Chatham' which may persuade the Germans at DARESALAM that the truce is no longer binding.[23]

However, it is unclear how much importance Aitken placed on this information although he claims to have discussed the matter both on the *Karmala* and later ashore. Capt. Caulfeild's opinion was clear: the landings at Tanga must be preceded by a formal announcement of its abrogation and a demand to surrender. Furthermore, he presented a plan made by Capt. Ingles, late of the *Pegasus*, which saw the force landing one brigade at Dar-es-Salaam and then the second at Tanga. Aitken declined to make any commitment, however, until he had had a conference in Mombasa. As his chief intelligence officer had been present during *Chatham's* negotiations at Dar-es-Salaam and on board the *Fox* since 26 October, Aitken was as up to date as he could be.[24]

That evening, the *Fox* and *Karmala*, carrying Gen. Aitken and his headquarters, entered the port of Mombasa while the rest of the convoy remained at sea out of sight of land. The following morning a conference was held ashore with the participants including Gen. Aitken and his staff, Capt. Caulfeild, the governor of British East Africa, Gen. Stewart, and the commander of the Protectorate forces. One important absentee was Norman King, now a major, who had not been invited despite his detailed knowledge of both the enemy colony and its principal officials.

The meeting appears to have been a vague and unsatisfactory affair with virtually no new intelligence being presented since the departure from India; Col. Mackay having proven himself singularly inept at intelligence or staff work.[25] Nevertheless, Capt. Meinertzhagen, his deputy, had been busy in India and had collected a reasonable amount of information. Despite Aitken's subsequent claims of having virtually no intelligence on Tanga and German East Africa, contemporary evidence counters this assertion. For example, 'Field Notes on German East Africa', over ninety pages long, was produced and distributed to IEF B in August 1914. This booklet was quite accurate and identified the strengths, locations and numbers of all the companies in the *Schutztruppe*. Furthermore, it provided some basic information on Tanga noting the shallowness of the harbour, the presence of seaside

30. HMS Chatham and Capt. Drury-Lowe.

cliffs and mangrove swamps. Finally, it quoted the main German daily of 5 August as saying:

> We will not give up a hand's breadth of German soil which is capable of defence, without a hard struggle. We cannot, of course, think of defending our open town against the guns of a hostile squadron; but whatever we consider we have the least chance of holding we will hold.[26]

All of the Intelligence reports from IEF C had been received as had the latest naval information from the SNO. Furthermore, Aitken had a newly commissioned intelligence officer, 2nd-Lt Ishmael, on his staff. This officer had been the assistant manager of a rubber plantation near Tanga for a number of years and knew the area very well. Although he helped to produce a report on the place, it appears to have made little impact on Aitken, perhaps as the former was a civilian and not British.[27] As well, he had Maj. A. Russell, a planter who had lived in the German colony, now acting as an intelligence officer.[28]

If more evidence was required, then a letter intercepted at Aden provided it. In it the German colonial secretary informed Governor Schnee that the coastal towns were not to be defended and that the defence of the colony would continue if such ports were lost.[29] This important information was transmitted to IEF B before its departure from Bombay while further reports of the enemy's likely reaction were generated from interviews of Indian civilians who had been in recent personal service of *Schutztruppe* officers. They indicated that the coastal towns would not be held although stiff resistance would be offered in the interior.[30]

If anything, over-confidence seemed to pervade the conference as Aitken dismissed the possibility of serious, indeed any, opposition and refused the offer of an experienced battalion of the KAR to act as a covering force.[31] There was doubtless a sense of rivalry as the Indian Army officers looked down on the African forces as only being fit for operations against tribesmen. This is despite the fact that a number of Aitken's officers, including one of his brigade commanders, had served with the KAR and knew their worth in bush warfare.

The main point of dissension was the standing of the truce. Clearly, by notifying the German authorities of its abrogation any chance of surprise would be dashed. From a military point of view, it was highly undesirable and Aitken expressed his concern about it. However, Caulfeild and Ingles stood firm and insisted that a separate warning had to be issued at Tanga – interestingly no one seems to have thought of consulting with the captain of the *Chatham* who had already declared the truce invalid in Dar-es-Salaam and was well within wireless range.[32]

This issue highlighted the lack of a unified command structure as Aitken had no authority over the naval forces and could not over-rule Caulfeild. However, he could have appealed to the Commander-in-Chief, East Indies, who now controlled naval operations in East Africa, or even delayed the landings until after the ultimatum had been delivered. His own instructions did not give any firm deadlines for landing and despite the material change to the situation he did not seek clarification from India.[33] His decision may have been influenced by his complacency about the German reaction and the knowledge that the bulk of their forces lay some eighteen hours away by rail in the Kilimanjaro area.[34] He also greatly underestimated the fighting power of African troops and particularly the *Schutztruppe*.[35]

On the other hand, the news from the *Chatham* that the main naval threat to the landings, the *Königsberg*, had just been found hiding in the delta of the River Rufiji was extremely welcome. With the German cruiser now cut off, this left only the *Emden* at large in the eastern Indian Ocean where it was well out of range of IEF B.[36] From a naval perspective, it was safe to start the landings.[37]

Having agreed to respect the breaking of the truce, Aitken now outlined his plan to the conference. The only extant records appear in the IEF B War Diary, which noted:

> The following line of action was decided upon: 'B' Force to land at TANGA, form Base there & work up USAMBARA railway; Gen. STEWART co-operating from VOI and LONGIDO. A small expedition to be sent, as soon after landing as possible, from TANGA towards VANGA, to co-operate with a detachment of 'C' Force now at GAZI.

Clearly, Aitken and Stewart had little grasp of the strength and determination of the enemy force or its redoubtable commander, as the plan went on to state:

> Should it be evident, after engagements at MOMBO & elsewhere on the railway, that the enemy's remaining power of resistance is inconsiderable, it be possible for Gen. STEWART to complete the subjugation of the MOSHI section without further assistance; in which case 'B' Force can withdraw to TANGA and commence second phase, via DAR-ES-SALAAM and the Central Railway, at a somewhat earlier date.[38]

This was also reflected in the belief that resistance would collapse before the German main body, which was correctly identified as being concentrated between Moschi and Mombo, could redeploy to Tanga. Indeed, although the immediate surrender of Tanga was presumed, little thought was given to the likely response of the enemy forces outside of the town, particularly as intelligence indicated that they would fight for the colony. Finally, the role of Gen. Stewart and IEF C was vague and ill-defined – he was to 'co-operate' from Voi and Longido towards Moschi. As Voi was some ninety miles from the Mombasa and Longido was a further 150 miles north-west of Voi, it would take him at least twelve hours to return to his command, issue orders and commence deployment, time would be very tight. As no preliminary orders had been sent ahead, either from India or the convoy, Stewart's first intimation of his new role came at the conference. Despite having less than thirty-six hours to the commencement of the landings, Stewart did not bother to telegraph ahead and chose to deliver the information personally on his return.[39] As will be seen, this was to have an important impact on the subsidiary operations in the north.

German Actions in October

The clash between Schnee and Lettow continued throughout the month of October, each convinced of the rightness of his own views. Schnee had always wanted to avoid the war, and when forced into hostilities, he wished to minimise the damage to the colony. Lettow, more bellicose and with a professional soldier's instincts, wanted to fight wherever possible and not give up any territory without a fight, especially key ports. He was also determined to protect Tanga as his entire Kilimanjaro position depended on the efficient functioning of the Usambara railway line. While the loss of the port would not directly cut off his troops, as a trolley line and road ran south from Handeni towards Morogoro, it would leave the British with a threatening base for further operations against the railway. He was also aware that the *Königsberg's* sinking of the *Pegasus* would have seriously weakened the truce in British eyes, a concern underlined by the *Chatham's* shelling of Dar-es-Salaam on 21 October.[40]

Despite Lettow's attempts to rebuff further negotiations with the British, he was overruled by Schnee in an exchange of telegrams in late October – nothing was to be done that would give the British a justification for shelling the towns. If the first battle had not been won, the *Kommandeur* was concerned about the health and efficiency of his troops as the ports provided the necessary accommodation and services needed to sustain a garrison in an unhealthy climate and Lettow wanted to keep his troops as fit as possible. Accordingly, Schnee modified his earlier instructions and allowed part of *II Batallion* to live in Tanga, provided that they discretely evacuated the town if a British ship arrived. He further stipulated that the *Bezirksamtmann* would retain full control of the town. Matters were to remain firmly in civil hands under his ultimate direction.[41]

Warning signs about British intentions also began to appear more regularly. Their operational security for the planned landings in German East Africa was generally poor. As one officer noted with dismay, ships were being loaded with crates clearly marked 'Indian Expeditionary Force "B" – Mombasa' while the destination of the force had been widely talked about for at least a month.[42] Whether these lapses reached the Germans is unclear, but they did receive unmistakable reports about British intentions through captured newspapers and letters. On 12 October, captured British agents spoke of potential landings at Dar-es-Salaam, Bagamoyo and Tanga. Their suspicions were further raised by wireless transmissions intercepted from stations in the Belgian Congo.[43]

German concerns were further aroused on 21 October by the *Chatham's* arrival in Dar-es-Salaam harbour and shelling what it thought to be the *Königsberg's* masts, hitting a disabled merchantman instead. This had the dual effect of alerting the Germans to the danger of landings while also reinforcing the governor's resolve to avoid any direct defensive measures that would lead to a British bombardment of the towns. But Col. Lettow was in no doubt and signalled Baumstark on the same day that a landing at Tanga was possible.[44]

However, in the last week of October, captured letters made it clear that a 10,000-strong Indian expeditionary corps was expected to land imminently. A direct warning about the probability of a landing at Tanga was signalled to Baumstark on 22 October. Armed with such persuasive information, Lettow made a personal visit to Tanga where he held a planning conference with Baumstark, the commander of *17 FK*, and the *Bezirksamtmann*, Dr Auracher, on 28 October. The former specifically questioned Lettow on what his response to a landing should be and was told that vigorous response was essential. The *Kommandeur* was well aware that he was instructing a civilian official to act in direct contradiction of the governor's orders and stated that he would personally assume all responsibility for the consequences of such action. The course of action decided, Lettow then left Tanga in his car, arriving back at Neu Moschi on 30 October.[45]

PLANS FOR A DIVERSIONARY ATTACK NEAR KILIMANJARO

British assumptions about the Germans were based on a belief that memories of the *Maji-Maji* rebellion would inhibit the Germans from concentrating their forces.[46] While this was partially correct, Lettow had managed to collect a strong force in the Kilimanjaro area with only small garrisons left elsewhere. However, with the Usambara railway, he possessed good operational mobility between the north-west and Tanga, provided that the line remained intact. On the other hand, movement between that area and the Central Railway including Dar-es-Salaam was slow, taking at least a week. From pre-war intelligence and Norman King's reports, the British were well aware of German railway capabilities and particularly that the journey between the two railheads could be done in about eighteen hours. Similarly, they had correctly identified that the bulk of the enemy force was located in the Kilimanjaro area while the threat of significant opposition at Tanga had been dismissed. What neither Aitken nor Stewart seems to have considered in any depth were Lettow's potential counter-moves, including a redeployment from Kilimanjaro to the coast. This failure to think the problem through would become particularly evident in the part played by IEF C.

During the conference at Mombasa, Aitken had given Stewart a supporting role in the north. Although it is not clear whether he expected the latter to 'co-operate' from both Voi and Longido, it is certain that at least one attack against the German main body was agreed. The Voi–Taveta approach was the most direct, but the thirty miles between the two places was a waterless plain. Stewart lacked sufficient transport to sustain an advance in that direction while being open to strong counter-attack. Further north at Longido, the situation appeared more favourable as it was isolated from the German main body by Mount Kilimanjaro itself. The first reason was that the country was open and suitable for mounted troops, being free of the tsetse fly that destroyed all domestic animals. Secondly, water supplies were known to exist on Longido Hill as they did on the British side at Oldoinyo Erok. Finally, a nearby branch railway line meant that it was relatively easy to support operations in the area.

Longido was about thirty miles north and west of the Kilimanjaro feature and consisted of a series of four major hills that straddled the international border. North of the hills was Lake Magadi, a large salt lake that was used for the extraction of soda ash. A railway spur ran conveniently from Magadi Junction to Kaijaido, from where tracks led south towards Longido. The most northerly feature, Emombarasha Hill, was about halfway between Kaijaido and Longido with Ingito Hill some twelve miles to the south-west. Oldoinyo Erok, a well-watered hill some five miles south-east of Ingito, marked the southerly British position. Longido itself lay a further twelve miles south of Erok and was separated by a waterless plain. It was quite elevated and frequently enshrouded by cloud and mist.

However, the aim of Stewart's operation was never made clear by Aitken. If no opposition was expected at Tanga, then the timing of IEF C's move was not important as there would no need to draw off German reserves. In that case, Stewart's force would simply capture Longido as a preliminary to taking the surrender of the enemy around Kilimanjaro. If, as seems more likely, Aitken wished Stewart to delay or prevent a German re-deployment to Tanga, then the attack would have to precede the landings. With the slowness of passing on information in the bush and then issuing orders, the enemy needed to be engaged at least twenty-four hours before the convoy arrived.

However, time for preparation was extremely short as Aitken planned to land on 2 November and Stewart did not return until the early hours of that day.[47] Stewart had already made some preliminary preparations by concentrating a substantial force, some 1,500 strong, at the camp at Oldoinyo Erok, by the end of October. With over 800 infantry and 350 mounted rifles together with a pair of mountain guns, the British believed themselves superior to the 400–500 estimated defenders of *Abt Kraut* who held the Longido position. Kraut was in fact considerably stronger, having four companies totalling some 660 rifles and six machine guns in good defensive positions.[48]

Given that he faced a twelve-hour train journey back to his headquarters, he displayed no sense of urgency as he chose not to telegraph orders ahead of his departure from Mombasa. Although the troops were in position, it would still take time for reconnaissances to be carried out and orders to be issued; and Stewart wasted much valuable time. In the end, the attack was to take place on 3 November, a day after the landings were due to have commenced. It would be a critical error.

5

THE ULTIMATUM
AND INITIAL LANDINGS

THE PLAN FOR TAKING TANGA

As the Mombasa conference broke up, with the plan having been made, a new and vexing problem arose for Gen. Aitken. The condensers of the battleship *Goliath* broke down and the ship had to remain at Mombasa for repairs.[1] This meant more than the loss of his most important source of fire support, but also a second naval vessel with which to control the ill-disciplined assortment of civilian troopships that made up the convoy. Furthermore, there was insufficient space on the *Fox* to accommodate the military commander and his staff, causing Aitken to choose to remain on the *Karmala*.[2] Although it seems not to have been realised at the time, this decision would have serious implications for the command and control of the landings as the only communications between the two key senior officers would be via a wireless link. Furthermore, the GOC did not send a liaison officer aboard the *Fox* to provide military advice about the landings.

Aitken now had to make an important decision. He had overcome his serious misgivings about the need to abrogate the truce and now one of his escorts was out of action. His troops had been confined to small and unpleasant troopships in tropical conditions for two weeks with little opportunity for exercise or training. His orders had imposed no deadline for the landings, but he believed that they should begin as soon as possible. Despite the significant changes to the original situation, he chose not to delay, with departure of the convoy being set for the afternoon of 1 November.[3]

That evening, Capt. Caulfeild produced the naval convoy order which was then distributed to all ships and force headquarters. Although it gave considerable coverage on the details of boat drills and convoy discipline, the most important part dealt with the denunciation of the truce. He anticipated that the expedition would rendezvous some fifteen miles off Tanga by 0600 hours on 2 November. The *Fox*, accompanied by three tugs as mine sweepers, would then sail into the harbour to

31. HMS *Goliath* – a breakdown of condensers prevented its taking part in the landings at Tanga.

deliver the ultimatum, while the *Karmala* acted as convoy leader on the roadstead. Once the German surrender had been accepted, the *Fox* would rejoin the transports, distributing its three naval pilots to the leading vessels, and then bringing the ships in successively. Tellingly, there was no mention of what actions should be followed should resistance be met or if the Germans failed to surrender.[4]

The order of landing had been determined by Aitken who wished the Imperial Service Brigade to disembark first together with the labour force, supply depot, force headquarters and messes. On the second day, he planned to land 27 Brigade with its four battalions, the mountain battery and the specialist railway troops. It is remarkable to note that neither the naval landing plan nor the military operation order emphasised speed of landing or the probability of opposition. Aitken's instructions went so far as to say:

> From reliable information received it appears improbable that the enemy will actively oppose our landing. Opposition may, however, be met with anywhere inland, and a considerable force of the enemy is reported to be in the vicinity of Vanga.[5]

Neither document specified the place or area of landing, but presumably they assumed that the lighters would be able to tie up alongside the jetty. Thus from the outset, the success of the entire operation depended on German capitulation with no contingency plans or other options in place. This represented an enormously complacent view given the fact that all the intelligence indicators pointed towards a robust German reaction to any landings. It was a dangerous presumption to think that the enemy would allow the British the uncontested control of the town before launching attacks thereafter.

The weakness of the British planning and the lack of urgency in landing was reflected in Aitken's operation order. It was a very sketchy document that lacked important information such as detailed timings, the formations to be used and fire support. Apart from the fact that the Imperial Service Brigade was to land first and seize the town of Tanga there was little guidance given – the main paragraph read:

> Brigadier-General M.J. Tighe, C.B., C.I.E., D.S.O. (Imperial Service Brigade), will form the covering party and will take up a position covering the town and port of Tanga.[6]

Ironically, more attention was placed on the administrative aspects of the landings than the vital tactical direction. For example, despite the orders noting the distinct possibility of opposition once ashore, it was planned to land the staff baggage, messes and base depot establishment on Day 1 while the whole of 27 Brigade would not start landing until Day 2. It also gave no indication as to the likely scale or determination of defenders.[7]

The radically changed situation that followed from the German rejection of the ultimatum should have resulted in modified orders, particularly as regards the enemy intentions. Little was done and it took until 1700 hours that evening to produce a two-page order that made no mention of resistance and limited Tighe's instructions to the terse phrase, 'The town of Tanga is to be seized to-night.'[8]

NAVAL ORDER AND COUNTER-ORDER

Unbeknownst to the GOC, further confusion was about to descend on the naval arrangements. Back in London, and despite the imminence of IEF B's landings, the Admiralty continued to be fixated by what it considered the urgent priority, that of the destruction of the *Königsberg*. That ship's sinking of the *Pegasus* had caused a rapid reappraisal of the balance of naval power and substantial reinforcements had been sent in late September. The *Fox* had been leading three other cruisers in the hunt for the enemy vessel, until it was detached to escort IEF B.[9] But, Churchill's consistent intervention into the details of ship movements and the lack of a proper war staff meant that a flurry of orders were sent directly to individual ships with the commanders-in-chief often being bypassed. One direct result was their failure to remember to order the abrogation of the truce, which it had been intended to take place before the expedition left its forward base.

The second was the focus on the *Königsberg* to the detriment of the assault on German East Africa. Although that ship was still at large and the possibility of linking up with the Emden could not be discounted, the Admiralty considered that the *Fox* and *Goliath* were more than sufficient to protect IEF B. As such, the landings were left to continue as planned. However, on 30 October, the day that the convoy arrived off Mombasa, the light cruiser *Chatham*, acting on the clues found during its visit to Lindi, located the *Königsberg*'s hiding place in the waters of the Rufiji delta, south of Dar-es-Salaam. While this meant that it was safe for the troops to land at Tanga, the news caused Churchill and his naval staff to focus almost exclusively on the enemy cruiser. On 31 October, they signalled Capt. Caulfeild to transfer into the *Hardinge*, while the *Fox* was to leave the convoy and assist in the blockade of the *Königsberg*. At the same time, Gen. Aitken was to be asked to provide troops in assistance of the operation.[10]

Such a change, on the eve of the landings, would have deprived IEF B of all its firepower as the *Goliath* was now not available. Furthermore, the *Hardinge* was not a proper warship, being lightly armed, and the loss of the *Fox* would deprive Caulfeild of the naval pilots who were essential to his plan. Most importantly, the Admiralty had forgotten that it had already ordered the *Hardinge* off to Mauritius in order to escort its garrison home. With a lack of clear priorities and poor staff work, chaos loomed. However, the transmission of these orders took some time and probably arrived after the convoy had left Mombasa. It is unclear whether they were missed in the excitement of preparing for battle, which seems unlikely, or whether Caulfeild turned a blind eye to them. Whatever the reason, they were ignored and the expedition continued on its course.[11]

THE ULTIMATUM AND INITIAL LANDINGS

The convoy arrived off Tanga at 0450 hours on 2 November and the *Fox* sailed in alone under a white flag to notify the authorities of the abrogation of the truce and to demand their surrender. However, it took the cruiser over two hours to reach the inner harbour and anchor owing to the navigation aids having been removed by the defenders and a fear of mines.[12] The Germans received their first notification of the invasion fleet at 0630 hours from an alert lookout at Amboni, who spotted the smoke from the convoy as it lay offshore.[13]

Initially, the Germans were uncertain of the cruiser's intentions as they had had several meetings under the terms of the truce. They had been informed of the presence of the transport ships outside the reef, but when the *Bezirksamtmann* and his interpreter arrived on the *Fox*, they were quickly made aware of the purpose of the visit. Caulfeild announced that Tanga was no longer considered an open town and demanded its unconditional surrender within an hour. Dr Auracher protested, noting that it would be impossible to make the return journey as well as conferring with his superiors in that time. Caulfeild relented and extended the deadline to $2\frac{1}{2}$ hours and stated that if the white flag was not raised by that time, he would begin shelling the town. The interview now at an end, the Germans made their way out of the captain's cabin only to be recalled by Caulfeild who threatened to shoot both of them if anything happened to his ship. He then demanded to know whether mines had been laid in the harbour and their exact location. Auracher declined to give any military information and was again threatened with shooting if mines were encountered. With these angry words, the meeting finally broke up with the Germans returning to their boat. Now aware of the British anxiety about mines as well as their absence in the harbour, as a deception measure, they made straight for shore, landing some three miles from the town before running all the way back to pass on the news.[14]

Immediately on his return to his offices, Auracher telegraphed both Lettow in Neu Moschi, and subsequently Schnee, of the British demands. He received the uncompromising order that Tanga was to be defended at all costs. He quickly ordered the evacuation of all non-combatants while all able-bodied males were to assist in its defence. This was hardly a formidable force, as most men had already joined the *Schutztruppe*, and amounted to barely twenty-five, each equipped with only twenty rounds of ammunition. The only other troops were the fifty *Polizei-Askaris* that had been permitted under the terms of the truce, but these were all young recruits with minimal training. The nearest reserves, the other two platoons of *17 FK*, were four miles away on defensive duties at Kange Station.[15] His civil duties now completed, Auracher then donned his uniform as a reserve officer and rushed off to join in the defences.[16]

Thus, by mid-morning the expeditionary force of nearly 6,000 fighting troops faced an opposition of a mere seventy-five barely trained and inadequately armed

32. HMS *Fox* – the flagship of the expedition.

33. Tanga Harbour looking towards the customs shed. Toten Island can be seen on the left and Ras Kasone is visible in the far distance on the right.

men with another 100 marching to their assistance. A landing at this stage would have almost certainly overwhelmed the defenders, no matter how determined and gallant their efforts. For the time being, the British were unable to land even a single company, thereby foregoing their overwhelming superiority in numbers.

Gen. Aitken remained ignorant of the development of events and was unaware that his force had been spotted shortly after daybreak and that the Germans were already redeploying their forces, however small, around the town. *17 FK* had started to move forward just after 0600 and the platoon in Tanga moved to occupy the promontory of Ras Kasone after Auracher's return.[17] Much further to the north, Lettow was waiting for further confirmation of British intentions before executing his riposte.

After an hour's wait and seeing that no reply was forthcoming, the *Fox* signalled its return to the convoy, which was still some fifteen miles offshore. She did not leave until 1045 hours and then, upon arrival, Capt. Caulfeild went into a conference with Gen. Aitken and his staff onboard the *Karmala*. The commanding officers had also been summoned from their transports, but as most of these lacked motor launches, it took some time to assemble on the headquarters ship. Thus it was early afternoon before the senior officers could be briefed on the new situation and revised instructions issued.

With the departure of the *Fox* and the move of the convoy to the south, it seemed to many that the British had left for another destination, probably Dar-es-Salaam. Nevertheless, *17 FK* took up defensive positions blocking the key approaches to the town, concentrating on the three small bridges that crossed the railway cutting. A strong patrol was sent out to gain contact with the enemy, but in view of the presence of the *Fox*, some 800 yards away, it prudently remained out of direct vision.[18] At the same time, Lettow forbore from making any movements south while Baumstark, further up the coast accompanying *16 FK*, decided not to enter Tanga for the same reasons.[19]

The German refusal to surrender clearly left Aitken nonplussed as he had no contingency plan to cover such an obvious possibility. Indeed, the operation order, which had been distributed the night before and had stated that no immediate opposition was to be expected, remained unaltered despite the complete change in the situation. Discussion then focused on suitable landing sites for the troops, which again had not been seriously considered or reconnoitred. On the naval side, Caulfeild's concerns about mines then dominated proceedings as he refused to enter harbour without a channel having been swept. Nor would he permit a direct landing on the harbour front unless covered by the guns of the *Fox*. This meant further delay in landing and dictated a beach out of direct view from Tanga.

This decision meant that the landing site would have to be somewhere along the long line of cliffs and mangrove swamps that extended southward from the headland of Ras Kasone towards Pangani. With the lack of preparations, the time for reconnaissance was very short and limited to a telescopic viewing from the *Fox* after its return from the negotiations. The only possible place was hardly ideal as it passed through a mangrove swamp before running into 20ft-high cliffs – they were scaleable, but were a definite hindrance to movement. Ironically, a junior intelligence officer with knowledge of the area had previously identified the same landing place, but little attention had been paid to him. Now christened 'Landing

34. Tanga Harbour as it looked under peacetime conditions.

35. Ras Kasone looking south. The mangrove swamps are apparent.

36. Ras Kasone as seen from SS *Nairung*. The heavy vegetation makes observation very difficult.

Place A', its only advantage was its concealment from direct observation from the town while its disadvantages were substantial. As the War Diary pointed out:

> It was, however, extremely unfavourable. The edge of the coral reef was about 500 yards from the shore, & lighters could not come closer, except at high tide; men had therefore to wade ashore, often falling into deep pools *en route* – and even the luckiest were wet to their waists; while the exits from the beach were few, narrow and deep.[20]

While a high tide was necessary to reach the shore, it also rendered the sandy beach less than 10ft wide. Once the escarpment had been scrambled, the area opened up briefly around the area of the 'Red House', a European bungalow, before being swallowed into the trees of the Tanga plantation. About 1,000 yards to the north, on the eastern edge of Ras Kasone, lay another planter's home, this one two stories high and dubbed the 'White House'. Further west and in full view of Tanga was the 'Signal Tower' which was used to communicate with shipping.

The Möhn Plantation was the next significant feature as it ran from several thousand yards south of the Red House north almost up to the White House. In the north, it was laid out with sisal, a spiky and sharp leaved plant that is a formidable barrier to movement, while in the south there were rubber trees, dense but with little undergrowth. In all cases, visibility was never more than fifty yards and in many places much less. There were two roads in the area, running north-east to south-west from the Signal Tower and the White House with a track starting about 500 yards south of the Red House. Additionally, a lateral road from the latter place connected the two northerly routes before they left the plantation proper. None were wide and all were vulnerable to ambush from the dense vegetation on either side.[21]

In essence, Gen. Aitken had been forced to land his troops at a site that was poor at best and then been faced with an advance through dense vegetation and limited visibility. After all the wasted time and lethargy that typified 2 November, it was a most unsatisfactory way to commence land operations after two weeks at sea.[22]

Aitken seemed unable to grasp the full implications of the German refusal to capitulate. Following the conference, his principal staff officer told an officer that, after landing successfully at Tanga, one brigade would advance up the Usambara railway while the other would clear the coastline towards Mombasa. When pressed about the enemy's intentions, he responded that Aitken was quite convinced that there would be no resistance and had asked the navy not to shell the town and damage their future accommodation.[23] For his part, once the revised orders were issued, Aitken retired to a deck chair reading a novel, seemingly unconcerned about the slowness of the disembarkation of his troops.[24] It was either a remarkable case of *sang-froid* or an inability to understand the seriousness of the situation.

More time was lost as the troops had to wait on board until the small boats conducting mine-sweeping operations had completed their task. Once this laborious operation was completed in mid-afternoon, the tempo of the landings was further reduced by Capt. Caulfeild's decision to bring in only three transports with the *Fox* before dark. Citing the fact that he had only three pilots familiar with the approaches, he left the remainder of the convoy at sea for the night.[25] This had the effect of slowing the rate of disembarkation very considerably and would have important effects later the next day.

The lack of urgency was further underlined by the slowness of getting the landings underway. The *Fox* led the three transports towards Tanga at 1500 hours although they did not reach their destination and anchor until an hour and a half later. The first beach party was sent ashore at 1800, just as darkness began to fall.[26] On the German side, the reappearance of the British fleet galvanised the *Schutztruppe* into action. Now sure that Tanga was the target, Lettow ordered his troops to concentrate at Neu Moschi as quickly as possible, leaving only a single company from each *Abteilung* to hold the line against IEF C. His reserve located at Neu Moschi consisted of *6 FK, 6 Sch K* and a platoon of *1 FK*; they were ordered to entrain immediately for the journey south. In the meantime, the few automobiles in the area were sent to pick up *Abt von Prince*, near Taveta, and to bring them to the railhead as quickly as possible.[27] The only blip in these arrangements was with *Abt Kraut* located in the north at Longido where a breakdown of telephone communications was to delay his orders to withdraw by twenty-four hours – a fateful pause as will be seen.

It was 1700 hours before serious activity began. The three leading transports, *Pentacotah, Jeddah* and *Karmala* carrying the 13th Rajputs, 61st Pioneers, and Force Headquarters and 2nd Loyal North Lancashires respectively, had anchored about 2,000 yards south east of Ras Kasone while the lighters had been brought up to them. The remainder of the convoy remained at sea as there were no buoys, the channel was difficult and there were only three pilots; in the circumstances Caulfeild believed that it would be impossible to bring the remainder in safely during darkness. Finally, a new operation order was issued to reflect the changed circumstances. It was extremely brief and limited itself to stating that the 13th Rajputs and 61st Pioneers under the command of Gen. Tighe would land as a covering party and seize Tanga that night. No mention of enemy activity was given.

If the GOC was slow and hesitant, at least Gen. Tighe had been making best use of the time available. He had summoned his commanding officers onto the *Karmala* at 0800 hours and had briefed them on his plan of landing. By early afternoon, he had confirmed his orders by signal and the lead elements, the 13th Rajputs and Brigade Scouts, were ready to move at 1600 hours. Unfortunately, a combination of darkness and a lack of familiarity with boats meant that the loading of the lighters took from 1745 to 2000 hours.

The method of landing was seriously handicapped by the nature of the approaches, and in particular the reef. As the lighters had no engines, they had to be towed forward by tugs which then released them just before the coral. They were expected to reach shore under their own impetus and assisted by passengers with poles. Insufficient attention had been paid to the state of the tides as low water was at 2130 hours.[28] Consequently, at 2230 hours, the leading craft grounded still some 500 yards offshore where the water was too deep to wade and fully equipped men were unable to swim ashore. Indeed, much of the Imperial Service Brigade's headquarters spent four hours stranded helplessly under bright tropical moonlight, before being rescued.[29] It was at this time that a small German patrol from *17 FK* spotted the stranded craft and opened fire from the cliff tops. Machine gun fire from the boats and a 6-in. round from the *Fox* was sufficient to silence the enemy, who prudently withdrew from their exposed positions.[30]

However, there were good examples of individual initiative. One officer of the 13th Rajputs, Capt. Seymour, had managed to swim ashore and reconnoitred a route to the lighters. On his return, he took the scouts and fifty men from each lighter ashore, equipped only with rifles and ammunition. This party then reached the beach at about 2315 hours and began to probe towards Tanga, meeting no opposition. The other lighters continued to struggle over the reef with many left stranded until the tide rose. In the meantime, smaller craft and ship's boats were sent to assist the larger vessels in off-loading their cargoes, but this was a slow and time-consuming process. It took up to four hours for the bulk of the vessels to make their way to the muddy beach and unloaded their wet and weary cargo.[31]

The commander of the Imperial Service Brigade was ashore by midnight and concentrating his troops as they landed around the Red House. By 0230 hours on 3 November, the whole of 13th Rajputs, the Brigade Scouts and four single companies of the 61st Pioneers had landed and patrols were being pushed to the west. Fifteen minutes later, the forward elements of *17 FK* ran into the British piquets but were quickly driven off.[32] IEF B was now beginning to move on its

37. The Red House and cliffs. Gen. Tighe based the Imperial Service Brigade here on 3 November.

38. The beach south of the Red House. It was muddy and narrow.

39. The beach used at Landing Place A. The troops climbed the cliffs near the steps at the left.

objective, but it had taken $8\frac{1}{2}$ hours from the belated beginning of the landings to assemble a sizeable force ashore. More than seventeen hours had elapsed from the expiration of the *Fox*'s deadline – things were moving very slowly indeed.

Throughout the night and next morning, Aitken and his staff remained on the *Karmala*, seemingly content to let events develop rather than to take charge. This is difficult to understand, given that the German refusal to surrender had dramatically altered the military situation. While he had conferred with Caulfeild at length in the afternoon, as soon as the latter returned to his flagship, Aitken could only communicate with him through the relatively cumbersome and slow method of Morse wireless transmissions. Matters were not aided by his continued failure to station a military liaison officer on the warship and the rudimentary ship to shore communications. Despite his misgivings, he considered that three battalions would be sufficient to land, seize the town and cover the disembarkation of the remainder of the force.[33] He was not alone in his complacency, as Brig. Wapshare actually suggested that it would have been better to wait for daylight before landing.[34]

LETTOW REACTS TO THE LANDINGS

For their part, the Germans were far from inactive. At the time of the *Fox*'s arrival, there was only one company, *17 FK*, near Tanga with two more companies a day's

40. A *Feldkompagnie* on the march to battle. The commander is mounted and the men march.

41. German *Askaris* on the train taking them to Tanga.

hard march to the north, with a further two deployed along the Usambara Railway. The bulk of Lettow's force, some fourteen companies, was deployed in the area around Mount Kilimanjaro, with his headquarters at the railway terminus at Neu Moschi some 150 miles from Tanga.[35] A further two *Sch K* were deployed defensively along the Usambara Railway with three more under Baumstark on the coastal area. As already seen, one platoon of *17 FK* was in Tanga with the other two at Kange Station preparing to march northward to the border. Both *15 FK* and *16 FK* were deployed further north, between Jasin and Tanga, while the understrength *4 Sch K* was guarding the railway a few miles to the west of the town. Interestingly, none of Baumstark's troops were regulars, all having been newly recruited since the outbreak of war.

On receiving word of the British presence and their ultimatum Col. Lettow immediately set about recalling a large proportion of his outlying forces and ordering them to concentrate on Neu Moschi and entrain for Tanga. Within an hour of receiving the warning, the first company was moving south along the single-track railway. Schnee had explicitly forbidden Lettow from fortifying Tanga, but that had not prevented his making an extensive personal reconnaissance beforehand. He had also made contingency plans in some detail with Auracher and Baumstark beforehand. Lettow refused to consider giving up the town without a fight and disregarded two telegrams from Governor Schnee ordering him not to defend Tanga proper (although they permitted defences outside the town).[36] The commander of *17 FK* was not to be alone for long as he was now in telegraphic communications with his superiors and learned that the staff of *II Batallion* and *16 FK* would be joining him before dawn on 3 November.[37]

6

THE FIRST ATTACK –
3 NOVEMBER 1914

THE FIRST PROBES AND INITIAL RESISTANCE

Just after midnight on 3 November, after extricating themselves from the clutches of the coral reef, the leading elements of the Imperial Service Brigade began to consolidate ashore. Patrols were sent out to locate the enemy while the officers pushed their bedraggled companies further inland. Brigade headquarters quickly established itself in the Red House with field telephone lines being laid to the forward units. On the beaches, the disembarkation staff set it up, ready to receive the expected reinforcements.

In the meantime, by 0030 hours, the energetic Capt. Seymour had pushed forward with a reconnaissance patrol to the eastern edges of the town where it located *17 FK*'s defences and machine guns situated near the railway workshops.[1] At the same time, the Germans were attempting to determine the size of the beachhead with small patrols lurking around the Red House.

With the whole of the 13th Rajputs and half the 61st Pioneers ashore by 0230, Gen. Tighe allowed his commanders several hours to reorganise themselves and prepare for the advance. There was a brief skirmish when the Indians bumped into one of *17 FK*'s patrols, but the Germans quickly withdrew and order was restored. By now impatient to begin, Tighe issued orders at 0430 hours to the commandant of the 13th Rajputs. They were instructed to push on to Tanga as quickly as possible in order to capture the railway station. One double company was also to take the post, telegraph and telephone offices, while cutting all wires except to the jetties. In the event that the railway station was not captured, the Rajputs were to inform Tighe by field telephone and he would in turn bring up the remainder of his force on a wide turning movement to the south to take it himself.[2] After the issue of battalion orders, the leading half of the Rajputs set off towards Tanga at 0515 hours.

Led by Capt. Seymour, the advanced troops pushed through the dense under-growth, passing the cemetery and reaching the drainage ditch east of the town. All

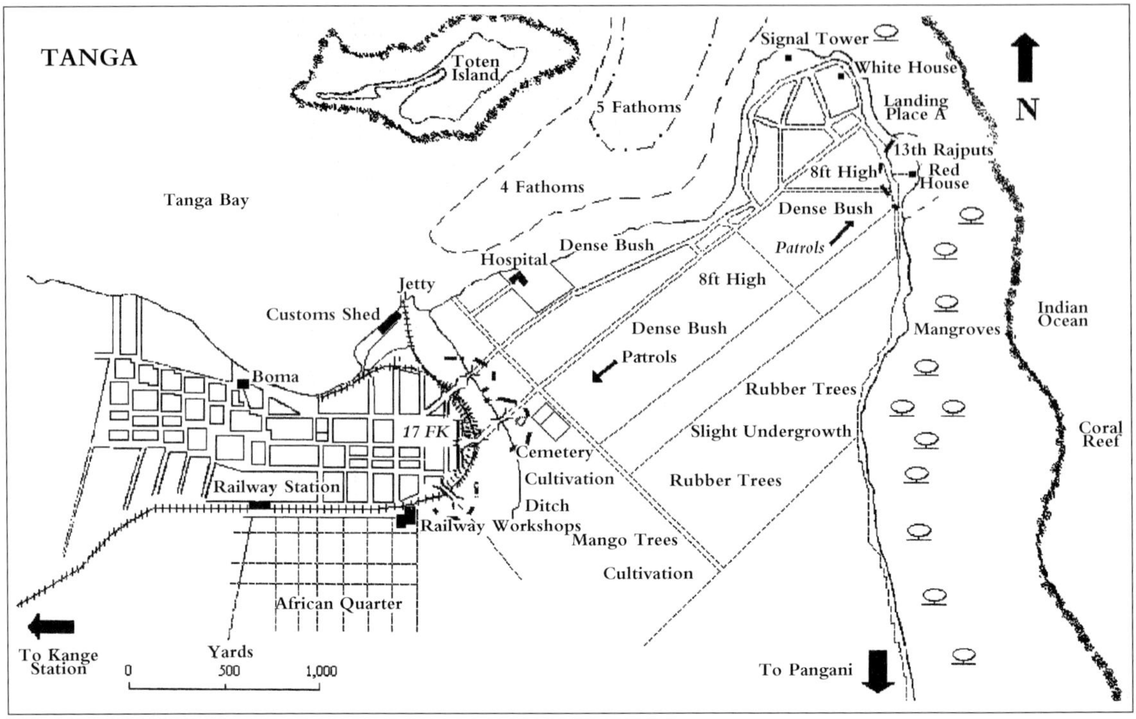

Map 6. The situation at 0030 hours, 3 November.

Map 7. The situation at 0700 hours, 3 November.

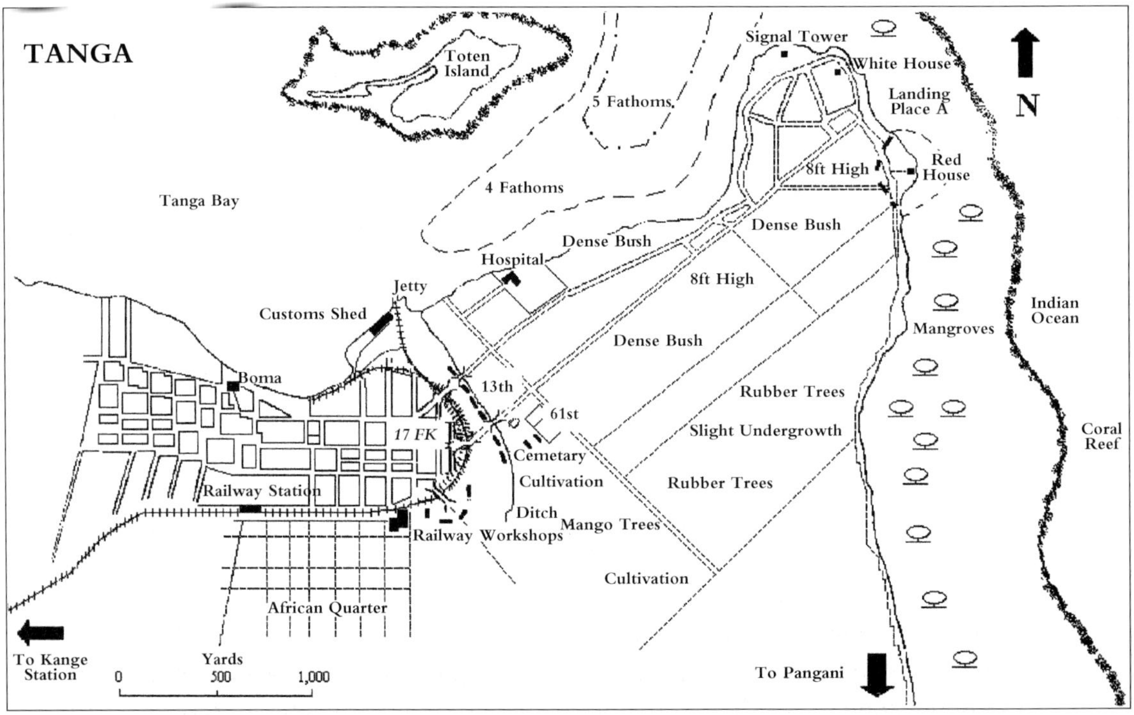

42. The ditch that was used by the Imperial Service Brigade on 3 November.

that could be seen was alternating cultivated fields and high grass with a number of huts scattered about. Visibility remained poor and communication between companies was difficult. There, at about 0545 hours, they came into view of town and suddenly encountered heavy fire. This was the main body of 17 FK, who were entrenched along the railway cutting some 300 yards distant. The weight of fire forced the Rajputs to go to ground and thereafter progress was very slow with movement being limited to crawling and short dashes. With targets being extremely difficult to identify in the vegetation, the commandant brought up his rear companies to extend the firing line. Owing to the firing and the poor visibility, this process took some time to carry out – at about this time the telephone line leading back to brigade headquarters was cut and communications were lost.

Tighe had had considerable experience of fighting in such close country, and hearing the sounds of heavy firing and now out of communications, he decided to move forward himself, bringing with him the remaining companies of the 13th and 61st.[3] Hurrying forward at the head of his troops, he arrived at the Rajput line about forty-five minutes later. After a personal reconnaissance, and seeing that the German machine guns were well sited, he decided to extend his line to the left, or south, and ordered the remainder of the Rajputs to move forward to take up positions along the ditch. Again, it took time, over thirty minutes, to carry out this manoeuvre with the result that by 0700 hours all companies were in position and exchanging fire. Opposite them, the heavily outnumbered but plucky *17 FK* was beginning to run out of ammunition, while the early morning dampness reduced the effectiveness of their black powder rifles and the smoke lingered to their front.[4] They were now outnumbered about four to one although they expected help to arrive soon.

As the battle raged, Seymour noticed that a number of troops were moving south out of Tanga toward the left flank of the Indians. Elsewhere, the situation remained confused with the limited visibility making it extremely difficult to locate the enemy. With the advance going nowhere, the commandant of the Rajputs ascended a small knoll with his adjutant in order to gain a better view. Suddenly, with the arrival of a third officer bringing in a message, the knoll was swept by machine gun fire. The results were devastating as the colonel was severely wounded and the other two killed outright. A few minutes later, one of the company commanders was badly wounded, further denting the soldiers' morale.[5]

Worst of all, the soldiers observed moving out of Tanga were part of *Abt Merensky*, the first German reinforcements to arrive. The troops of Lettow's reserve, *6 FK*, *6 Sch K* and a platoon of *1 FK* had made the 150-mile journey from Neu Moschi in about fifteen hours in open rail cars. They had arrived at Kange Station at 0630 hours, just as the battle was beginning to intensify and immediately forced-marched the four miles forward. Now to the rear of *17 FK*, Merensky was preparing to commit his companies to the fight. Lettow's initiative in planning and executing a rapid redeployment was about to pay dividends.[6]

Fifteen hundred yards to the rear, the disembarkation staff remained out of communications with Tighe. Fortunately, they had good links with the *Karmala* which remained close off shore. Shortly after 0600 hours, Brig.-Gen. Malleson, commanding the lines of communication, had received an urgent message from the 13th Rajputs asking for reinforcements, but as none had yet landed, there was nothing he could do except repeat the message to the ship. This was especially exasperating as the remaining two double companies of the 61st should already have landed and he could see the empty lighters tied up to the transport with no sign of activity.[7]

The deteriorating situation ashore also woke up the staff on board the *Karmala*, for at 0630 hours and a day early, the 2nd Loyal North Lancashire was warned to prepare two companies for landing. This went against the planned landing tables, but as the British battalion was on the headquarters ship and the rest of the Imperial Service Brigade was further out, it was the best solution to the problem.

Just behind the firing line, Tighe was oblivious to these developments. The 13th Rajputs had suffered painful losses and were showing distinct reluctance to move forward in face of the heavy fire. With his brigade still halted only several hundred yards from the railway, he decided that it was time to deploy his only reserve, the three single companies of the 61st Pioneers. Once again, the move forward through the bush was very difficult and they emerged from the western edge of the rubber plantation at 0700 hours. There they came almost immediately under effective fire, but pushed forward, in echelon formation, through the crops and tall grass towards the exposed left flank of the Rajputs.

So far, the renewed advance was effective. However, on being ordered to assault a group of enemy riflemen to their front, some men of the 61st refused to follow their British company commander and remained in their positions. This caused considerable consternation to Tighe for at the same time, about 0730 hours, a strong German counter-attack was developing on the vulnerable left flank. As the remainder of the 61st advanced towards the ditch that marked the British front line, they were raked with heavy machine gun fire before *17 FK*, now almost without ammunition, launched a sharp counter-attack onto the their left flank. This led to an intense fight in which several attempts by the Pioneers to storm enemy machine guns were repulsed with considerable loss, including two officers and many men. The Germans pressed their attack that was only finally halted by a brave stand by a British officer and a soldier from brigade headquarters who each shot down a number of their opponents. Unable to advance further and without ammunition, *17 FK* retired towards Tanga, its delaying mission successfully achieved. They had gained sufficient time for the leading elements of *Abt Merensky* to take up the line and who were now almost ready for their counter-attack.[8]

The coming of daylight had also altered the situation for the better, as with the immediate area of Ras Kasone cleared of enemy, Capt. Caulfeild decided to commence landings near the Signal Tower, at Landing Place B. These beaches were free of mangroves and could be reached by lighters unimpeded. This meant that disembarkation was significantly smoother than the night before while daylight eased the problems of loading the lighters.[9] However, it would be some time before large numbers of troops could be landed and could do little to relieve the pressure on the Imperial Service Brigade. Ominously, the disembarkation staff noted that a number of men had begun to stream back to the beaches. Members of both forward regiments were found lurking about the Red House and its environs, with many very reluctant to go back to the firing line. Many seemed to be exhausted, both morally and physically, and rounding up the stragglers was all that the staff could do.[10]

With the immediate threat from the front relieved, Tighe soon had greater worries to consider. It was clear that the enemy was growing stronger while the condition of both Indian battalions was worsening, both in numbers and in morale. By 0800 hours he was concerned as to whether his troops would hold any further; the answer was not long in coming as Merensky's troops began to charge on the southern flank. Faced by a strong enemy, largely invisible but highly audible through bugle calls and cheers, both the 61st and 13th began to fall back in some disorder. Tighe had already decided to withdraw back towards the beaches, but his hand was forced by the strong counter-attack. The firing was intense and one of his staff officers was killed trying to reach the commanding officer of the 61st with orders. Tighe himself arrived to find the 13th already falling back in disarray with demoralised sepoys abandoning their positions and returning to the beaches.[11] However, he was to have some good fortune as the third double company of the 61st which had managed to board its lighters at 0800 and finding a gap in the reef, made its way ashore by 0820. This much-needed sub-unit was then immediately sent forward to join its fellows.[12]

In the thickly cultivated terrain, the reduced 61st found it impossible to reform their line until the rubber plantation was reached, but even then heavy German pressure kept forcing them back. The 13th continued to fall back despite the brigadier's best efforts to make them stand and fight. However, demoralisation was not complete as the British and Indian officers continued to try and rally the men, a number of whom responded. Within half an hour, at 0830 hours, the Germans had reached the line of the hospital where they were halted by the fire of the newly arrived company of the 61st Pioneers who had immediately marched towards the fighting.[13] While all of this was underway, the *Fox* had entered the inner harbour and anchored in view of the town with the aim of marshalling the transports. On receiving word of the situation ashore, but lacking identifiable targets, the ship was asked to fire anywhere that was 1,500 yards in advance of the Red House. Accordingly, it fired a number of rounds at about 0915 hours with shells falling indiscriminately into the buildings, including the hospital, which accidentally received a direct hit. The naval gunfire was completely ineffective at halting the enemy whose momentum had effectively been checked by the timely arrival of the reserve company.[14]

The situation was now slightly less precarious as the fourth and final double company of the 61st came ashore at 0945 hours, their landing having been delayed

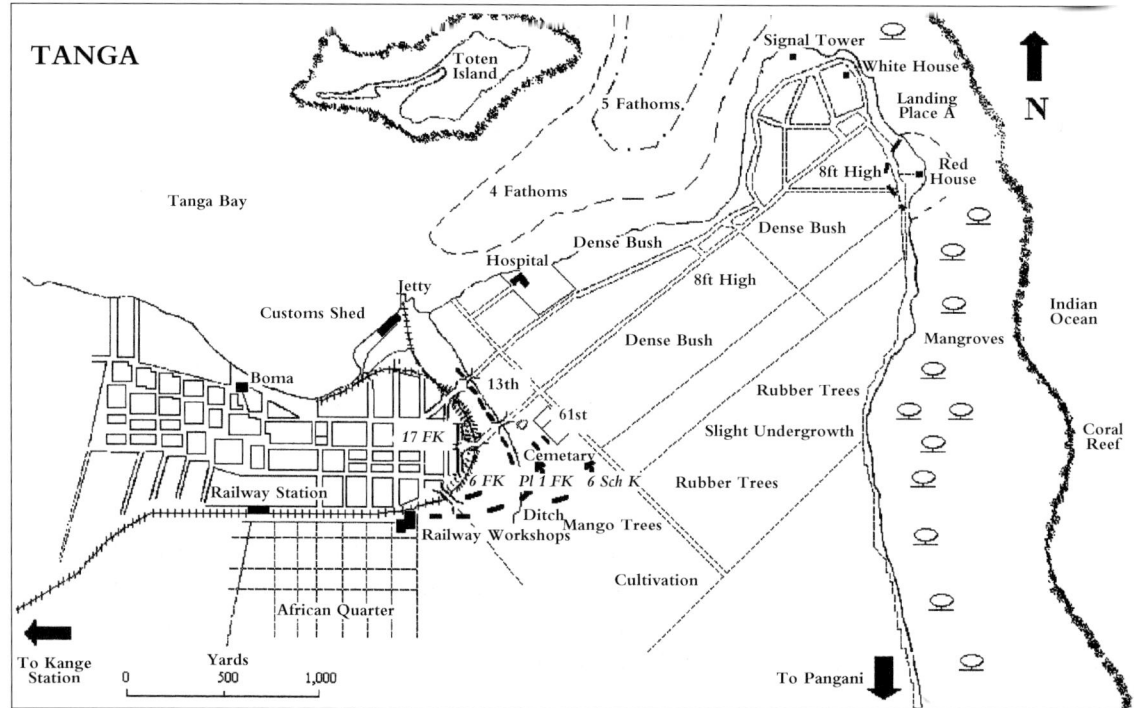

Map 8. The situation at 0830 hours, 3 November.

by being stranded on the coral reef on the falling tide.[15] Tighe quickly pulled his forces in to the area of the Red House and established a makeshift perimeter. He pressed for reinforcements as his troops were physically exhausted, some having had no sleep for twenty-four hours. Malleson urged his headquarters to expedite the landing of the 2nd Loyal North Lancashire, whose first two double companies landed at 1000 hours. The two battalions tried to reorganise themselves as best they could while the landing of further reinforcements was underway. Two hours later, a degree of order had been restored and the whole of the British battalion was ashore and taking up the front line.[16]

TIGHE CONSIDERS HIS NEXT MOVE

The command situation was also muddled, although this was through no fault of Tighe's. The initial landing plan had been based on the premise of an unopposed landing and sought to bring in support troops and the civilian workforce almost immediately after the first battalion. This meant that in the first wave only the 13th Rajputs belonged to the Imperial Service Brigade as the 61st Pioneers were actually divisional troops whose main purpose was to start the development of the base facilities. The unexpected landing of the North Lancashires, who were 27 Brigade troops, was due to their being on the *Karmala* and being the most convenient to put ashore quickly. The end result was that the brigade's troops and the divisional troops became intermingled.

Tighe now considered his next move. While the situation was serious, it was not disastrous; casualties had been heavy, but by no means overwhelming. The 61st Pioneers had suffered three officers and forty-four men killed, twenty-six men wounded and a further one officer and nineteen men missing, while the 13th Rajputs had three officers and thirty-five men killed with four officers and sixteen men wounded. The 2nd Loyal North Lancashire was completely intact.[17] The most pressing problem was the breakdown in morale and loss of offensive spirit. Tighe thought it unwise to risk a second rebuff when strong reinforcements were at hand. He sent Brig.-Gen. Malleson back to the *Karmala* to brief Aitken personally while also sending a strongly worded signal at 1200 hours:

> Troops dem[oralised] and wouldn't face. If they had charged position would have been won. Ran on German cheers… Both regiments unreliable and useless… Consider at least four Bns. are necessary; i.e. three NEW Bns… Inadvisable move out with N. Lancs alone.[18]

The combination of losing surprise and the inability to disembark quickly had altered the British superiority in numbers quite considerably. Through swift thinking and rapid action, the heavily outnumbered *17 FK* had been substantially reinforced. Several machine guns and a spirited defence of the railway cutting had halted a battalion and a half's advance; more critically most of the Imperial Service Brigade's offensive power had been lost within several hours' battle. What should have been a reasonably quick and successful attack against a limited defence had now turned into a much more deliberate slogging match with both sides adding reserves as quickly as they could. As the Loyal North Lancashire arrived, the balance of forces stood at twelve British companies as opposed to three and half German.

Ironically, during the disorder of the British forces, the local commander had abandoned the town of Tanga on the afternoon of 3 November. Capt. Baumstark, the local commander, lacked confidence and he had decided to withdraw his troops in the town back to Kange Station where they would regroup. He signalled Lettow:

> Bombardment of Tanga has commenced. No. 17 Company and two Moschi-Companies, which have been in action since early this morning, are retreating to Kange, where I have taken up covering position with No. 16 Company. Intend to take up further covering positions at Pongwe and Ngomeni.[19]

This was significant, as both the latter places mentioned were stations further to the west of Kange; in essence, Baumstark was proposing to abandon Tanga and fight a delaying action inland. Lettow was unwilling to give up so easily, especially as he had received a separate message from the town informing him that the British had been pushed back to the hospital and that the bombardment had consisted of six rounds. He sent his own orders to his staff and subordinates in the Kilimanjaro area, 'Enemy landed strong forces at Tanga. Expedite sending of troops.'[20]

It was nearly 1230 when Malleson arrived on board the *Karmala* to brief the force commander on the unsatisfactory situation ashore. As the remainder of the Imperial Service Brigade was now beginning to land there was little that Aitken could do except to let the Navy carry on with the process of disembarkation. The pilots changed ships and by early afternoon, the next three ships came into the harbour which was now declared free of mines. This meant that the third beach, Landing Place C, which was closer to Tanga and had a steeply shelving beach that was ideal for lighters, could be used.

With the *Fox* covering the two new landing sites, the pace of disembarkation began to accelerate. The 3rd Kashmir Rifles left the *Bajora* at 1400 hours and were completely landed at the Signal Tower by 1600. There, they linked up with the 2nd Kashmir Rifles and the four companies of the 3rd Gwalior Infantry at 1800 hours where they formed an outpost line from the sea to the boundary with 27 Brigade.[21] Gen. Malleson landed with them, and on realising that Beach C was actually in front of the outpost line, he ordered them to secure the immediate area until relieved. There they remained, undisturbed, throughout the night.

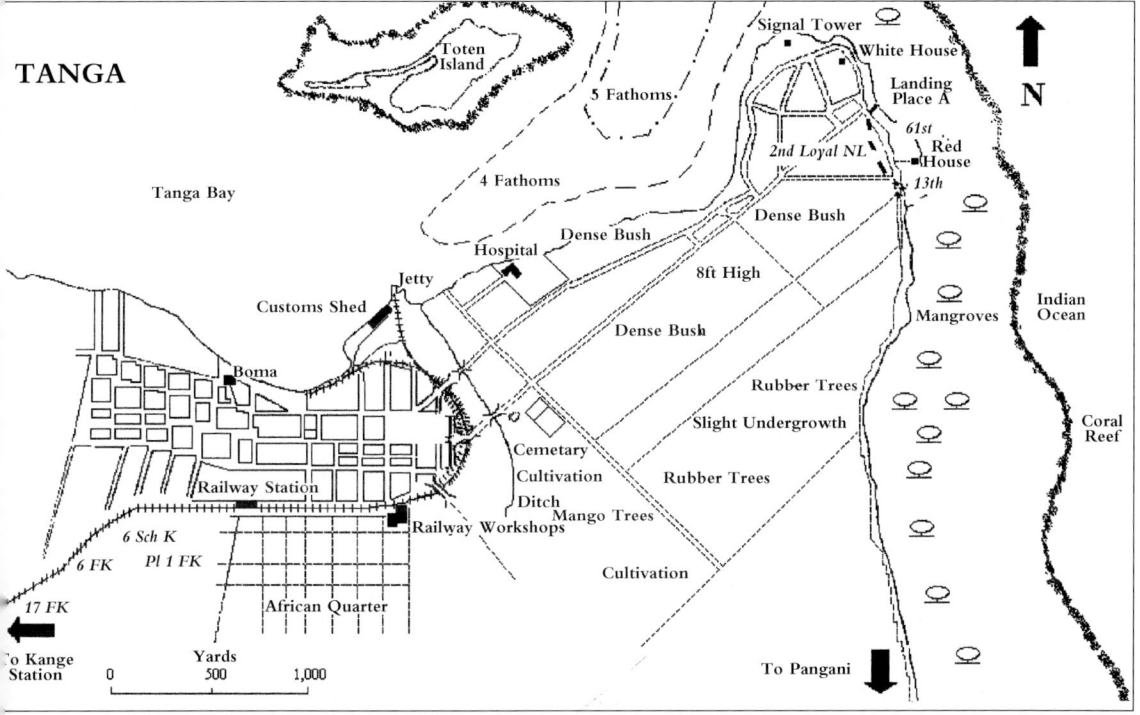

Map 9. The situation at 1200 hours, 3 November.

Finally, at 1700 hours, Gen. Aitken and his staff left their ship to direct operations ashore. On arrival, he found the scene confused amongst the detritus of the morning's disastrous attack. The beaches were crowded with the beach parties, stores and newly arriving troops. Making his headquarters at the White House, he began to reorganise his base staff, sending them to the Signal Tower and leaving a company of the Gwaliors at each of the beaches. The force war diary seemed to anticipate criticisms of the organisation by noting:

> The position occupied by the Force was by no means an ideal base for protracted operations. There was, however, no choice. It would have been impossible to force a landing on the exposed TANGA sea-front, for the inner harbour only admitted three or four transports, lighters could not have got near the gently shelving beach, and to have attempted a landing in open ships' boats, either by day or by the light of the nearly full moon, would have been very dangerous & difficult.[22]

Aitken was able to see for himself the demoralised state of Tighe's leading units, although the remaining two were in good order. It was clear to him that more fighting power was required and he did not wish to risk a night attack. While this decision may be justified, neither Aitken nor Tighe appears to have used their reinforcements to conduct any meaningful patrols to establish contact with the enemy. Instead, units were ordered to dig trenches and improve the perimeter defences

43. The White House. Gen. Aitken used this building as IEF B headquarters.

44. A panoramic view of Tanga Harbour from the western side of Ras Kasone. Landing Place C is visible on the left and the hospital can be made out in the middle distance on the left-centre.

around the landing sites. There was no evidence of aggressive spirit and most seemed content to hold for the night. This was to be an extremely costly error as the British completely missed the German evacuation of Tanga and enabled Lettow to re-occupy it without a struggle early the next morning.

If the build-up of British forces was improving, it was still far from ideal. It was dark before the last of the Imperial Service Brigade was landed, leaving three battalions of 27 Brigade still on their transports. Initially, they were ordered to land during the night, but the order was quickly countermanded and disembarkation was postponed until the next morning.[23] Officially, the reason was the lack of pilots, but Aitken revealed shortly after the battle that:

> I had not dared to disembark them the night of the 3rd–4th as I was afraid of a night attack. I thought it more likely the Germans might attack at dawn and I did not want troops to be caught disembarking as we had found a better landing place, marked 'B' on the Plan, also another marked 'C', both all right by day but dangerous at night when the Fox could not see to shoot.[24]

This left over a third of his fighting power out of reach, and he does not seem to have considered using the less suitable Landing Place A in order to work through the night. Later, with his self-imposed delay in landing the final three of his eight battalions, disembarkation of the infantry was not completed until nearly mid-morning the next day.[25]

THE GERMAN RE-OCCUPATION OF TANGA

Baumstark had received Lettow's emphatic signal to re-occupy Tanga at 2100 hours that evening. Accordingly, he marched his now five and a half company strong force back to a point three miles from the now empty town.[26] If the British were settling down to hold their limited gains, the Germans were actively re-establishing themselves throughout the night of 3–4 November. Arriving himself at Kange Station at 0300 hours on 4 November, Col. Lettow found similar confusion amongst his own troops. It was unclear whether the British had occupied Tanga or were making any further advance as Baumstark was still outside the town and had made little effort to gain further information.

Lettow immediately ordered his subordinate to prepare to move forward in readiness to reoccupy the town as quickly as possible. Then, in order to gain a clearer grasp of the situation, the German commander mounted a bicycle and pedalled into Tanga ahead of his own troops. Reaching the hospital and walking down to the beach, Lettow decided to reoccupy as quickly as possible. Sending a rider back, he instructed Baumstark to send his battalion, now including

Merensky's reinforcements, into the town together with newly arrived *Abt von Prince* (7 and *8 Sch K*).[27]

The rest of the night was spent in the re-deployment of troops and the preparation of defences. Two of Baumstark's companies, *6* and *16 FK*, were placed along the railway cutting facing east with the remaining three and a half companies positioned to the right rear of *16 FK* in the African quarter. Well behind these forward defences, he positioned the two companies of *Abt von Prince* as a reserve. His plan was to entice the British into attacking the main defences on the edge of the town and then to defeat them with a strong flanking attacking from the right. For security, patrols were also pushed out to the south. With the further arrival of *13 FK* at 0900 hours on 4 November, the reinforced German defenders now numbered $8\frac{1}{2}$ companies or a total of 935 rifles and fifteen machine guns. Facing them were about five British battalions, numbering approximately 4,000 troops with six machine guns, although only 2,600 rifles were considered to be effective.[28]

As the remaining three battalions of 27 Brigade were in the process of landing, the British superiority in numbers was growing rapidly.

7

THE SECOND ATTACK – 4 NOVEMBER 1914

SUBSIDIARY OPERATIONS AT LONGIDO

While Gen. Tighe's attack was miscarrying at Tanga, both sides were active in the area north of Mount Kilimanjaro, near Longido. As decided at the Mombasa conference, Stewart was due to 'co-operate' from that direction in support of the landings. Seeing that the Germans had occupied strong positions on the slopes of Longido mountain, the British commander decided to make a night approach march followed by a light frontal holding attack combined with two flanking columns. The aim was to seize the enemy's water supply and cut off their retreat. The attack was launched at dawn on 3 November, just as Kraut was receiving his orders to concentrate on Neu Moschi prior to moving to Tanga. The plan miscarried as one of the flanking columns struggled to find the water holes in the dense bush and soon ran into determined German counter-attacks. The other column had difficulty keeping direction in the thick early morning mist and came under heavy fire as it lifted. The position was further worsened by the stampeding of the mules carrying the force's water and stiffening German resistance. After fighting for much of the day, the British were stranded high on a mountain ridge without water and with numerous casualties. Withdrawal was the only option and by dawn on 4 November, the attackers had been driven back to their initial camp. The attack cost the British fifty-three casualties as opposed to the Germans' forty.[1]

But Kraut was unhappy with his situation as his supply of food was nearly exhausted. Moreover, he was heavily outnumbered. He asked for permission to withdraw back towards Kilimanjaro; instead he was brusquely ordered to hold Longido further.[2]

It is difficult to discern the point of this operation, coming as it did a day after the landings at Tanga. Stewart's force lacked the strength to take on Lettow's main body. Nor did it have the transport resources to conduct a general advance. In the circumstances and with the focus on capturing the seaport, it made much more

45. East African Mounted Rifles below the formidable summit of Longido.
This photograph was taken in 1915.

46. Taking cover near Longido. Taken in subsequent operation in 1915.

sense to launch a diversionary attack that would prevent the redeployment of troops from the Kilimanjaro area. Given the slowness of communications and the time needed to issue orders, it would have been much more useful for Stewart to have started his move at least twenty-four hours before Aitken, not the other way round. The attack at Longido with perhaps a feint towards Taveta might well have discouraged Lettow from sending the bulk of his troops southward to Tanga; certainly it prevented three out of Kraut's four companies from redeploying. Equally a move along the coast from the border at Gazi towards Jasin would have placed pressure on the Germans that would have assisted the landings.

As it was, the operation was too late to attract Lettow's attention while also being poorly executed. Had Stewart telegraphed a warning order immediately after the conference in Mombasa rather than waiting to make the twelve-hour rail journey to Nairobi, more thorough preparations and a more timely attack might have taken place. Instead, the attack on Longido was a double failure; it did not divert sufficient troops from attacking IEF B and it was unable to capture the enemy position. Once again, the British approach to fighting had been exposed as amateurish and lackadaisical.

THE PLAN TO SEIZE TANGA

The sharp rebuff to Tighe's troops on the morning of 3 November had punctured any illusions, if they still persisted, of an easy capture of Tanga. It was clear that

47. East African Mounted Rifles near Longido.

48. Casualty evacuation by stretcher. This was slow and exhausting for both
bearers and casualty.

enemy reinforcements had arrived and that being so, others might be on their way.
If so, time was of the essence and a rapid build up of strength essential. As a great
deal of time had already been lost, landing the remaining three battalions of 27
Brigade as rapidly as possible was necessary for a decisive blow to be launched. Here
Aitken's mood swung from complacency to worry. Not knowing of the German
withdrawal, he considered that a German dawn attack, particularly around the
exposed beaches of Landing Place C was a distinct possibility. It was here that Aitken
again wasted more valuable time and gave his opponent breathing space. Instead of
sending strong security elements to regain contact with the enemy and keeping the
initiative, he kept his force huddled around the beachheads in a state of fearful antic-
ipation. Furthermore, he declined to use either Landing Place A or B; the difficulties of the former had been made evident, but even if slow, it was still useable.[3]

As a consequence, the twelve hours of darkness were wasted and the disembarkation of the remainder of 27 Brigade only resumed after 0600 hours on 4
November. Coming ashore at Landing Place C, the move was completed efficiently,
but the last troops only reached shore at 0930 hours. The 63rd Light Infantry, the
98th Infantry and the 101st Grenadiers moved from the beach directly inland to take
up their places behind the outpost line.[4] It was now forty-eight hours after the
expiry of the ultimatum and twenty hours after the defeat of Tighe's advance.

With these preliminary moves underway, the GOC conferred with his brigadiers and formulated his plan for the capture of Tanga. There were now two brigades totalling some eight battalions available for the attack. Of these, the 13th Rajputs and 61st Pioneers were considered too shaky for main effort, but were deemed suitable to act as a reserve. Deducting these two regiments, he still disposed of twenty-four double companies and twelve machine guns although only two of the latter were in the Imperial Service Brigade. He distrusted the 63rd and sandwiched them between the 101st Grenadiers and 2nd Loyal North Lancashire, both of whom he knew well, while placing the 98th Infantry, who he had been told were sound, to the 63rd's rear.[5] This still left him with twenty companies together with ample firepower in the form of the two 6-in and eight 4.7-in guns of the *Fox* and the six 10-pounder pack guns in 28th Indian Mountain Battery. While the defenders possessed three more machine guns than IEF B, they had no artillery and only a third of the effective infantry.

In making his plan, Aitken made a crucial decision about his fire support. He was very concerned about the effects of the thick vegetation on the mountain guns.

> The mountain battery was not landed – firstly because the dense bush, & rubber & massive plantations, with their deep furrows, would have seriously hampered the advance of the battery & restricted their view; and lastly because of the delay that would have been entailed by their disembarkation on the very unsuitable beaches.[6]

Instead, he chose to leave them on the *Bharata* and to prepare to engage from the ship's decks. This was a serious limitation as the depth of the harbour was insuffi-

49. The 98th Infantry bringing stores ashore at Landing Place C.

cient to enable the vessel to come in close enough to enfilade the railway cutting or the streets of the town. Furthermore, the events of the preceding day had made it obvious that the dense bush made the observation of targets, except those along the shoreline, almost impossible. Aitken also chose not to land forward observers while the communications between troops and vessels was tortuous; telephone line was to be laid from the forward units back to the brigade and force headquarters and then to the Red House and Signal Tower. From there, visual signals would be made to the ships to indicate targets. At best, this was a fragile system as lines were frequently cut in battle and the passage of information was slow and cumbersome.[7]

The guns of the *Fox* also promised to deliver strong fire support from the inner harbour, but the shallow water prevented it from coming beyond the four fathom line. Like the mountain guns on the *Bharata*, the gun crews could see virtually nothing. If there was little to be done about the cruiser, at least the mountain guns could be landed, escorted forward by infantry and brought to bear in the direct fire role, something in which they were well rehearsed.

Having decided upon his fire support, Gen. Aitken directed that both brigades would advance in extended line, side by side. The Imperial Service Brigade was to be on the right (north) with two battalions leading and one in support with 27 Brigade on the left with three battalions up and one in support. The general

50. SS *Bharata* with 28th Mountain Battery on the deck. The vegetation makes visibility very difficult.

51. Tanga and the hospital from the position of HMS *Fox*.

52. A modern view of the hospital.

53. An Indian Mountain Battery firing in the open. It shows clearly that the mountain guns were designed for direct fire.

reserve, at the GOC's personal disposal, was the 61st Pioneers, and would move behind the Imperial Service Brigade. The intent was to advance through the plantations towards Tanga and upon reaching the enemy defences, the Imperial Service Brigade would engage and fix the defenders while 27 Brigade would sweep around their southern flank and envelope the town from the rear. Frontages were narrow at 200–300 yards per battalion with the men virtually shoulder to shoulder. The plan depended on close touch being maintained by flanking units as well as accurate navigation, both difficult tasks in thick bush.[8]

The Imperial Service Brigade formed up forward of Landing Place C, with its right along the shoreline and then past the so-called 'Askari Road' to its left-hand boundary. The 2nd Kashmir Rifles were on the right with the half battalion of the 3rd Kashmirs, reinforced by a company of Gwaliors, on the left. The remaining three companies of 3rd Gwalior Infantry were left to secure the landing sites. To the south, or left, 27 Brigade extended from its neighbouring brigade south-eastwards into the Möhn Plantation. It deployed 2nd Loyal North Lancashire on the right flank with the 63rd Light Infantry in the centre and the 101st Grenadiers echeloned to the left rear, so as to provide a degree of flank protection.[9] Despite the thickness of the bush and the lack of visibility, Aitken believed that the four parallel tracks leading towards the town would keep the force correctly orientated. Finally, the 2nd Loyal North Lancashire was ordered to direct the advance with all other units keeping alignment with them.[10]

The operation order was distributed to units between 0930 and 1015 hours and H-Hr was set for 1200. This meant that the advance would start at the height of the day's heat, but the GOC wanted the troops to have lunch before starting. Time was also needed for the briefing of sub-units and the preliminary move to their start positions. Finally, all troops were in place and IEF B was set to commence full battle.

THE ADVANCE BEGINS

While these British preliminaries were underway, the Germans continued to prepare for the expected attack. Now disposing of nearly nine companies totalling about 935 together with fifteen machine guns, Lettow was still outnumbered by the approximately 5,500 British and Indians, a quarter of whom were now shaken. *Abt von Prince*, with 7 and 8 *Sch K*, largely composed of experienced reservists, had arrived during the night, while a further experienced regular company, *13 FK*, had

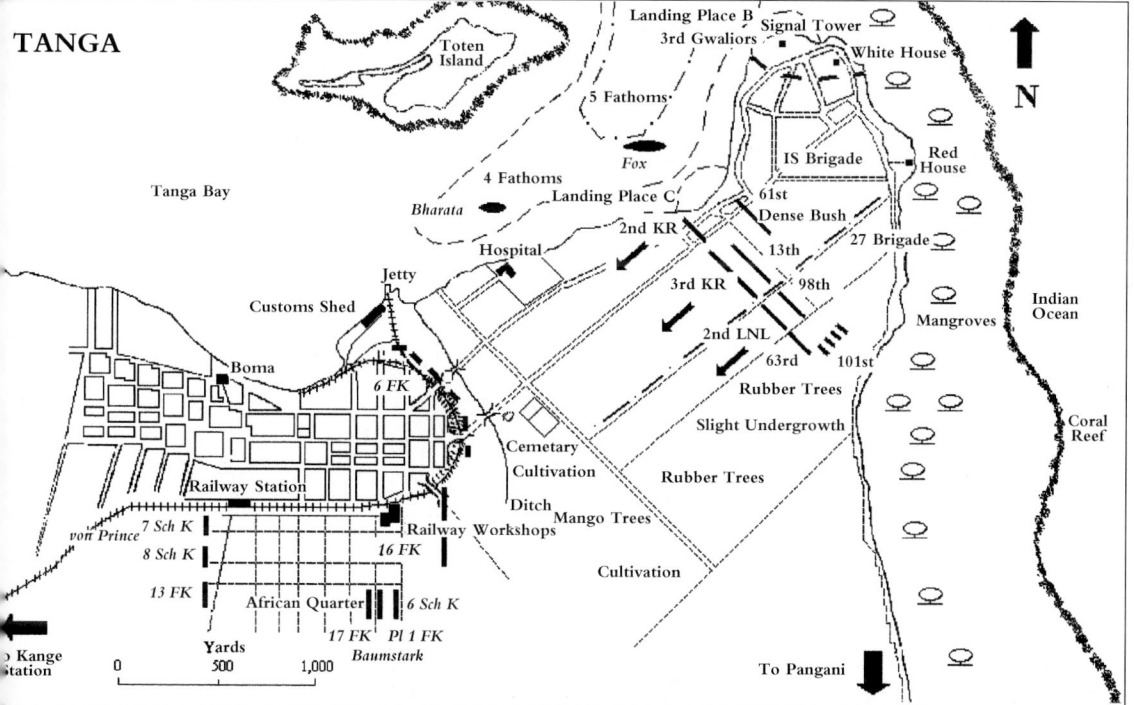

Map 10. The situation at 1230 hours, 4 November.

reached Kange by 0930 hours on 4 November. Lettow had conducted an extensive night-time reconnaissance and was now fully in command of the situation with Baumstark as his deputy. With the original garrison and the subsequent reinforcements deployed according to his plan, he was ready to defend Tanga. He was still heavily outnumbered, but his machine guns were well emplaced, houses had been prepared for defence and morale was still good.[11]

The day was blazing hot and the sun beat down remorselessly on the unfit and tired troops. The move through the plantations was unopposed, but very slow and difficult. Despite having only covered about 1,800 yards, many of the troops had exhausted their water bottles and were affected by the heat, a number being overcome. Keeping two battalions, let alone two brigades in extended line, was proving impossible in the dense vegetation and units began to adapt their formations. While unavoidable, the rate of advance began to vary perceptibly.

The first major setback occurred when the 63rd Light Infantry was attacked by a swarm of enraged bees. This disrupted the battalion's advance and it took some time to gather the scattered troops. While seemingly a trivial incident, bees were to play a significant role at Tanga as they attacked without discrimination. Their stings were especially virulent, and when disturbed the whole hive would attack any humans unlucky enough to be in the way. They made even battle impossible and everybody fled to avoid them. One unlucky British warrant officer manning his post was stung over 500 times and into unconsciousness; he was only saved from capture when a final sting aroused him and he made his way back to his unit.

After the battle, fantastic and ridiculous stories emerged about the Germans unleashing 'trained' bees onto the unsuspecting IEF B. The truth was rather more prosaic as bee keeping was common around Tanga. There were a large number of wooden bee hives suspended in the trees and the bees were disturbed through a combination of high firing and the cutting down of trees for defence material. The Germans also suffered from several attacks and at one point, an entire machine gun section was put out of action. The African bee was not to be underestimated.

As the 63rd struggled to regain its composure, the line of attackers reached the western edge of the rubber plantation. It was here, just as the attackers were about to enter the high grass and fields where the previous day's battle had been fought, that serious gaps appeared. At 1300 hours, being about 1,200 yards from the enemy, the 2nd Loyal North Lancashire noted that they had lost touch with the 3rd Kashmirs on the right. Their commanding officer halted the advance and consulted with Gen. Wapshare, who had come forward to view the situation. The battalion was instructed to wait until the stragglers caught up while the brigade was ordered to shift about 100 yards to the right in order to close up the gap. Further north, the Imperial Service Brigade started moving again after half an hour as the 3rd Kashmirs tried to catch up with the 2nd battalion, which had gone ahead.[12]

The troops of 27 Brigade remained static until nearly 1400 hours when the move forward was resumed. Plunging into the high grass, the brigade line began to bend as the North Lancashires began to outpace the more heavily laden and less fit 63rd who were suffering from having spent a month onboard ship. Farther back, General Headquarters followed up with the reserve in the slow and laborious advance.[13]

As the British force struggled forward, the Germans were lying in readiness to meet their attack. Their defences were based on the deep railway cutting to the east of the town with machine guns and strongpoints covering the three bridges. Working through the night, the *Schutztruppe* had fortified a number of buildings with windows boarded up and loopholes created. *6 FK* held the line from the sea to the southern edge of Tanga, where *16 FK* then took over forward of the railway workshops and the African quarter to the south. Echeloned slightly behind its northern neighbour, *6 Sch K*, followed by *17 FK* and then finally half of *1 FK* which marked the German right flank.[14] Small patrols had been sent forward with the occasional engagement that had almost no effect on the British.

As IEF B was sweating its way towards Tanga, Gen. Aitken decided to land nearly 3,000 civilian porters and labourers so as to be ready move into the town.[15] They were intended to carry loads for the troops as well as to do manual labour

54. A modern view of the railway cutting. It is quite deep with lots of vegetation on either side – a formidable obstacle when defended.

around the port, but with Tanga still in German hands and although the distances involved were short, they were of limited use. Furthermore, as they had absolutely no experience of military operations, they were liable to panic and run at the first sound of gunfire.

THE FIGHT FOR TANGA

First contact came at 1430 hours, when the leading elements of the Imperial Service Brigade came into sight of the railway cutting. The 2nd Kashmirs were immediately engaged by *6 FK* and the Indians promptly returned fire. After a number of short rushes, the battalion was halted by the weight of fire. Tighe sent forward three single companies of the 13th Rajputs from the support line to increase the pressure. Concurrently, the four single companies of the 3rd Kashmirs pushed ahead in order to link up with its sister battalion. On coming under effective fire, the attached company of 3rd Gwalior vanished from the field of battle although the Kashmiris valiantly fought on.[16]

27 Brigade had its baptism of fire almost at the same time as its northern neighbour. The three leading battalions came under rifle and machine gun fire from the forward German positions about 100 yards beyond the western edge of the rubber plantation. The 2nd Loyal North Lancashire was initially engaged from the centre of the cultivated area and were forced to go to ground. The machine guns were then called forward to the firing line where they began suppressing the well-concealed defenders. Supported by small arms fire, the companies pushed forward by a series of short rushes. It was very difficult to locate the enemy and on several occasions the Loyals were raked by friendly fire from other units. In the centre, the 63rd had also been held up by German fire, but showed much less aggression and many of the men would not go forward despite the entreaties of the officers. On the far left, the 101st Grenadiers came under sporadic fire and detected some enemy movement against its own left flank. Apart from reinforcing the vulnerable side, the battalion continued to skirmish forward without serious problems.[17] Across the 27 Brigade front, on the flanks, the Loyal North Lancashire and the Grenadiers were pressing forward determinedly while the centre held by the 63rd had stalled. Behind them, Gen. Wapshare was close at hand with the reserve battalion, the 98th Infantry.

At 1500 hours, and hearing the increasingly heavy firing from the Imperial Service Brigade, Gen. Wapshare ordered the British battalion to move further right and join in the attack. He also instructed the 63rd and 101st to conform to this movement, thereby closing the gap, but also ignoring his instructions to envelop the town from the south. The move exaggerated the existing gap between the Lancashires and the 63rd who, by now, were suffering badly from the heat and showing a reluctance to close with the enemy. Difficulties in navigation ensured that the message only reached half of the 63rd's companies and the remainder, together with commanding officer, continued to move straight ahead. Far to the left flank, the 101st did not receive Wapshare's revised orders at all and carried on their original axis.[18]

The British battalion was soon in the thick of the fight alongside the Kashmiris and engaging the increasingly outnumbered defenders. It was now its turn to feel the impact of the bees as one machine gun was temporarily put out of action and a number of troops badly stung. Elsewhere, shortly after 1600 hours, the 63rd, on coming under heavy machine gun fire from their front and being outflanked, quickly disintegrated. Despite the valiant efforts of its British and Indian officers to maintain control, the bulk of the soldiers were seen streaming to the rear. As the commanding officer later reported:

> The men with us had already fallen back and as the enemy were now working round our left rear the machine guns were sent back to a more suitable and less exposed position. With the exception of the gun detachment I regret to say I did not again see my men till I reached the morning's rendez-vous at about 7 p.m.[19]

This exodus was a major blow to Wapshare as a third of his manpower had suddenly disappeared. Orders were sent to the 101st on the extreme left of the brigade line to close up with the North Lancashires, who were now heavily committed to the fighting on the eastern edge of Tanga, but these appear never to have arrived. In the meantime, that battalion was fiercely engaged south of the railway workshops. The commanding officer went looking for the 63rd and found they had disappeared. He then attempted to get the 98th to move forward to fill the gap, but this was done reluctantly and not fully enough.[20]

While these events were underway, behind the firing line, the 98th Infantry had suffered a painful attack from a large swarm of enraged bees, as did Gen. Wapshare himself.[21] The battalion had been completely disrupted and although it was eventually rallied, it was badly shaken by the experience. Now needed to plug the hole left by the panic-stricken flight of the 63rd, the 98th were unsteady and showed a reluctance to close with the enemy.

In the north and in the confusion of battle, troops of both Kashmir battalions and the Rajputs had become intermingled. Several companies of the North Lancashire soon joined them and a fierce firefight ensued, supported ineffectually by the mountain guns afloat in the harbour. The weight of numbers showed and the 2nd Kashmir Rifles, soon joined on their left by the half battalion the 3rd Kashmir Rifles, drove 6 FK back to the cutting and kept the defenders under heavy pressure.[22]

By 1530 hours, the situation on the eastern edge of Tanga was confused and the scene of bitter, close-quarter fighting. On the north on the right of the British line along the shoreline, the 2nd and 3rd Kashmir Rifles had taken the railway cutting and broken into the town itself. Mingled with them were three companies of the

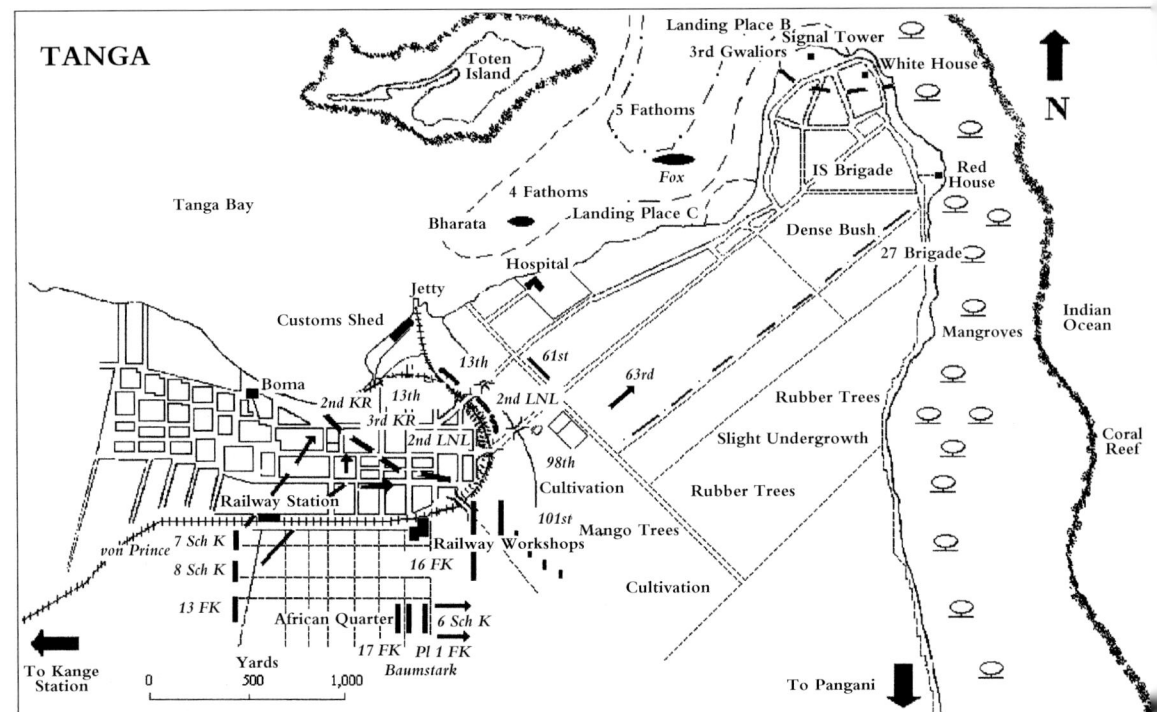

Map 11. The situation at 1515 hours, 4 November.

13th Rajputs and elements of all the 2nd Loyal North Lancashire's companies. Further south, the remainder of the British battalion was engaging the enemy south of the town while on the far flank the 101st Grenadiers was advancing in isolation toward the railway workshops and trying to close the gap in the line. The 63rd was no longer effective and the 98th was only taking their place slowly and without enthusiasm.

On the German side, the situation was far from favourable; *6 FK* was under serious pressure from the combined Kashmiri-Rajput attack and had been forced to withdraw from its positions along the railway cutting and back into the town. *16 FK*, south of the town, was also fully engaged by the advance of 27 Brigade. Very rapidly, the bulk of *17 FK* was diverted to the reinforcement of these two forward companies, leaving only a platoon in reserve. Worse, a number of the newly recruited *Askari* were running away from the Indian attackers.

At 1500 hours, Col. Lettow, realising the considerable danger to his left flank in the town, changed his plans and despatched *Abt von Prince* with two companies to support the embattled *6 FK*. He also ordered Capt. Baumstark to commit his reserve companies to the support of *16 FK* and to extend the German line to the south.[23] The critical moment for the defender's battle arose at about 1515 hours, when the Kashmiris turned *6 FK's* left flank reaching the Kaiserhof Hotel and the 2nd Loyal North Lancashire pushed past the left wing of *16 FK* and entered the town. A local platoon counter-attack had been halted by heavy British fire from the direction of the harbour – the threat to the German left wing was unmistakable.[24]

Tom von Prince was a most unusual character as his name might suggest. He had a British father and a German mother and spent much of his early life in Britain. He wished to pursue a military career, but was unable to gain admission to the British Army and decided to try his luck in Germany. There, he was admitted to a cadet college, ultimately being commissioned in the Prussian Army. After a varied career, where he served with Lettow at the *Kriegsschule*, he had come out to East Africa in the late 1880s, where he had fought in the wars of subjugation. He had rapidly gained a name for brutality as he participated in the systematic destruction of the Wahehe tribe's farmlands.[25] For his military exploits, he had been ennobled by the Kaiser and added the honorific *von* to his name while Africans nicknamed him *Bwana Sakkarani* (Master drunk with battlelust). He then became a planter in the Usambara district, but retained his fame and notoriety. In the urgent circumstances, von Prince was just the man to call upon.[26]

At this moment, von Prince launched his counter-attack using *7* and *8 Sch K* to relieve the pressure on *6 FK*. Advancing up the streets and using the upper stories of the buildings to sweep the open ground, the main blow fell on the companies of the 2nd Loyal North Lancashire. With *7 Sch K* leading, von Prince led his troops forward against the weakened and unsupported British.[27] Close-range house-to-house fighting ensued with the Germans making effective use of their machine guns. The shock of the counter-attack coupled with the lack of British fire support and co-ordination told heavily on the North Lancashires who began to take numerous casualties. Similarly, the Kashmiris fighting in the town were cut off from the British troops while the railway cutting behind them was frequently swept by machine gun fire. It was here that most of the battalion's casualties were suffered.[28]

Worryingly for Gen. Aitken, the events of the previous day appeared to be repeating themselves. Stragglers were observed making their way back to the landing sites in a demoralised and panic-stricken manner. By 1600, numbers were increasing, mainly it seemed from the 63rd, joined half an hour later by a company's worth of the 61st Pioneers. Between 1630 and 1700, staff officers estimated that 600–700 men of various units had collected in the rear, many of whom were cowering in the jungle. It was exceptionally difficult to rally them and to take up proper positions.[29]

Meanwhile, as the heavy fighting in the built-up areas continued, the 101st Grenadiers were fighting a lonely battle on the southern flank. Running into heavy fire from trenches south of the railway, the Indian troops were soon faced by the appearance of reinforcements from *II Batallion, 1 FK* and part of *17 FK* and later *4* and *6 Sch K*. Like their opponents they found advancing through the dense undergrowth extremely difficult and the companies soon became intermingled. However, pausing briefly the commander of *17 FK* managed to sort out the confusion and get the companies advancing again.[30]

27 Brigade was now dangerously split with its units scattered over a large frontage. At 1630 hours, Gen. Wapshare had ordered the 98th to move towards Tanga in order to support the heavily engaged 2nd Loyal North Lancashire, but the former

unit showed little enthusiasm for the attack. One company of the 98th retired to the rear and the remainder held firm and would not go forward.[31] This left the two battalions at either flank to fight isolated, piecemeal battles against strongly rein-forced defenders.

The Imperial Service Brigade was also concentrated in the north, with the bulk of its units still fighting off the German counter-attacks in the town. Both Kashmiri battalions and half the Rajputs had done well to break in, although casualties were beginning to mount. South of the railway cutting which was still very dangerous to cross, the remainder of the Rajputs held the line, with their machine gun section doing much good work. At 1545 hours, Tighe had asked the *Fox* to engage, but firing was quickly stopped after hitting the German hospital and some of their own troops.[32]

Gen. Aitken now faced a difficult situation. Two of 27 Brigade's battalions were ineffective while the other two were fighting largely independent battles on either flank. The Imperial Service Brigade, reinforced by half the North Lancashires, was under heavy pressure from von Prince's counter-attack and it remained difficult to push troops across the exposed railway cutting. The mountain battery and naval gunfire had been completely ineffectual although he still had the 61st Pioneers under his direct control. A crisis in the battle had emerged.

Further German Reinforcements Arrive

The Germans hoped to force a decision from the British as further reinforcements from Neu Moschi were still on the way. The long-expected and much-needed *4 FK* was still *en route* by rail. Faced with the lodgement in the town and having committed both *Abt von Prince* and *II Batallion* to counter-attacks, Lettow now had only *13 FK* in reserve. He was growing increasingly concerned as the young recruit *Askari* were wavering from the intensity of the enemy's fire. Unable to wait further for *4 FK*, and having stopped the enemy's progress in the town, he decided to launch *13 FK* at what he considered the decisive moment in the battle.[33]

Marching south of the railway and town, this company was sent against the left flank of the 101st Grenadiers at 1545 hours. The appearance of fresh and deter-mined troops was an unpleasant surprise for the now greatly weakened Grenadiers. Unsupported, and outflanked, the isolated battalion was forced back. By 1600 hours, the British left had given way and 27 Brigade was now in danger of being outflanked. The sudden arrival of *4 FK* at 1640 hours put further pressure on as it cut behind the advancing *13 FK* and struck north-east toward the centre of the British line. Aitken had lost telephonic communications with Wapshare on the left, and decided to start bringing back his line towards the hospital.[34]

The Germans had now fully regained the initiative. Their counter-attacks had stopped the British in the town and had finally turned the southern flank. Already

55. A 6in gun on HMS *Fox* firing.

56. SS *Bharata* with 28th Mountain Battery near the hospital. Despite the battle being underway, the gunners have no targets to engage.

57. A modern view of the centre of Tanga. Von Prince fell near the colonnaded building.

Map 12. The situation at 1640 hours, 4 November.

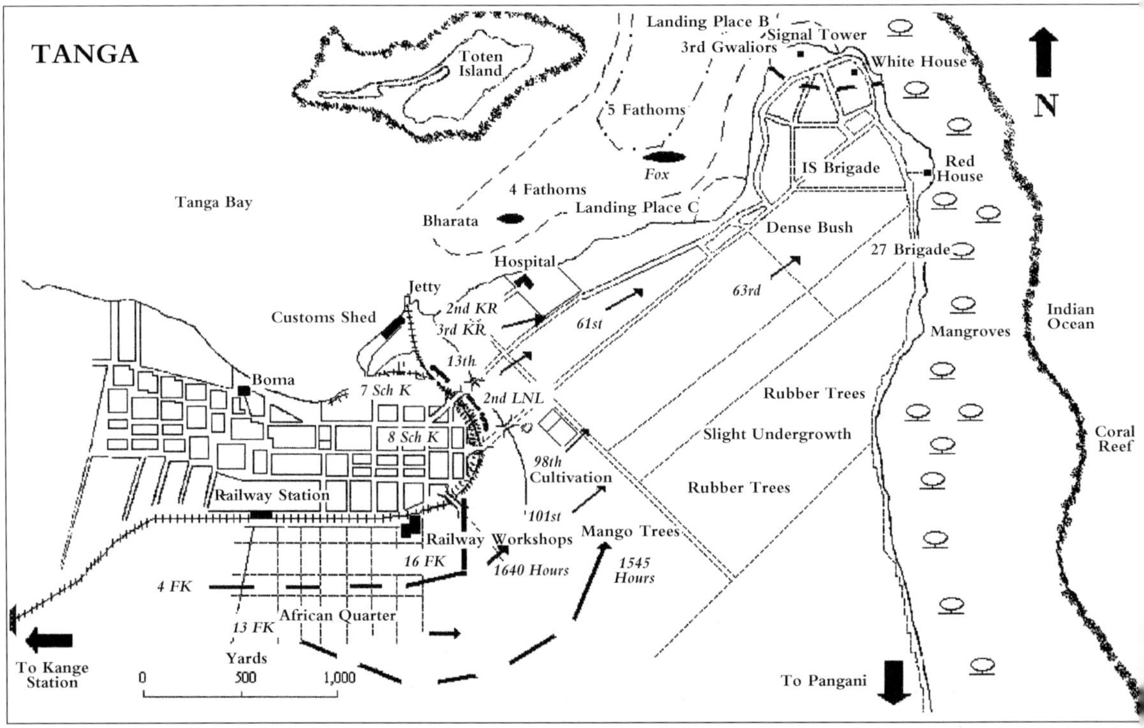

faced by the collapse of two of his battalions, Gen. Aitken's own reserve, the 61st Pioneers, now failed him and disintegrated. His fighting power severely impinged, the German advance forced Aitken to re-shape his line drastically. He ordered 27 Brigade to retire to the north and east, forming a line along the Askari Road facing south. The Imperial Service Brigade was pulled back to the area between the railway cutting and the German government hospital, facing west, this hasty defensive position at least protecting his hitherto open left flank.

THE BRITISH LOSS OF NERVE

If the situation in the forward areas was grim, the beaches were in a state of chaos. Fleeing soldiers streamed back toward the landing places despite the efforts of the staff to stop the tide. The situation was worsened by a sudden firing and subsequent panic by the unarmed carriers and followers who were supporting the fighting troops. Untrained civilians with no experience of battle and exhausted by their exertions in the bush, they dropped their loads and ran for their lives. The beach staffs did their best to restore order and discipline but it was a virtually impossible task, with equipment, ammunition and people everywhere.

Aitken, now well forward, witnessed the collapse of much of his force and decided to break off the attack for the day.[35] Considering the lack of water and the disorder of his force, Gen. Aitken ordered it to dig in east of the town for the night. Gen. Tighe was placed in command of the forward area while Gen. Wapshare was sent back to sort out the situation at the beaches.

The command group reached the White House after dark where they conferred about the next steps. The situation seemed grim as there were large numbers of wounded men with confusion everywhere and the troops very nervous. A further German attack was expected, and the rear area was in a state of turmoil.[36] Initially planning a midnight bayonet assault on the town, Aitken's brigadiers discouraged him from such an action as they doubted that their troops were capable of responding. Reviewing his options, Aitken realised that further reinforcements would not be forthcoming and his position was short of water, although not dangerously so. More importantly, he believed the majority of his force was now unfit for further offensive operations and that his reliable units had suffered too many casualties to be able to effective. Not knowing the size of the German force and fearing a further disaster if he remained, he decided to withdraw to a more compact beachhead perimeter.[37]

On the other hand, Col. Lettow was savouring the chance to inflict a decisive defeat on his opponents. However, he too was to be let down by his troops. While he was on the southern flank, preparing to co-ordinate a further attack by his counter-attacking force with that of the troops in the town, a bugle call sounded the order to withdraw. Baumstark had lost his nerve again and had instructed his companies to leave their hard-won positions and begin to pull back to Kange Station once more. It is not clear who gave the call, but Baumstark personally confirmed the order at 1800 hours and the company commanders were quite clear about their instructions.[38]

By the time he discovered the error, the town, which was being heavily shelled by the British, had been evacuated by the *Schutztruppe*. Without a means of quickly recalling his force and thinking the British planned a renewed attack, Lettow decided to abandon the town and fight from further west along the railway line. For a second time, the Germans had left the prize unguarded and the British failed again to notice. This was only partially redeemed by a message from Kraut at Longido – his troops had stopped the British advance there and his position was secure.[39] Co-operation from IEF C, late as it was, had failed; now it was IEF B's turn to admit defeat.

8

THE WITHDRAWAL ON 4 AND 5 NOVEMBER 1914

As darkness fell on 4 November, IEF B was holding an 'L'-shaped position around the government hospital and the troops were resolved to dig in for the night. Further back at the White House, Gen. Aitken was examining the possibilities for the future. Ostensibly, the situation seemed bleak as after some initial success in breaking into the town, his attack had faltered before being driven back by fresh German reserves. Several of his battalions had broken while two others had suffered heavy casualties. Despite these setbacks, he still had some strength as half his force had fought well and his mountain battery was still available for landing with the *Fox* able to protect the approaches along the seafront. His force had taken a hard knock, but it was not yet totally defeated. In the circumstances, he considered launching a night attack under moonlight as providing the final opportunity for fulfilling his mission. The biggest uncertainty would be the strength of the German response and whether the attackers could beat off the expected counter-attacks.

If he had used his best remaining troops and acted vigorously, it might have succeeded as, unbeknownst to him, Baumstark's lack of resolve had caused his troops to evacuate Tanga for a second time. The town now lay largely empty as the weary defenders trudged back to Kange Station. Once again, the British commander's failure to send out patrols or to try to remain in contact with the enemy meant that the opportunity was never even realised, let alone acted upon.

Aitken may have been hopeful, but his subordinates were much more pessimistic about renewing the battle. Tighe was very unhappy with the performance of the 13th Rajputs and the 61st Pioneers, considering them unlikely to withstand the strain of further fighting. On the other hand, Wapshare was equally unenthusiastic about the 63rd and 98th Infantry, whose failure to attack had led to heavy casualties amongst his good units. Finally, the views of Gen. Malleson, the inspector general of communications, painted a dark picture of the panic and loss of discipline of the stragglers collected around the beachhead. Against these thoughts must be set Aitken's own view of his force – he considered the Madras troops as 'the worst in India'.[1] However, the 101st Grenadiers had fought hard and suffered for

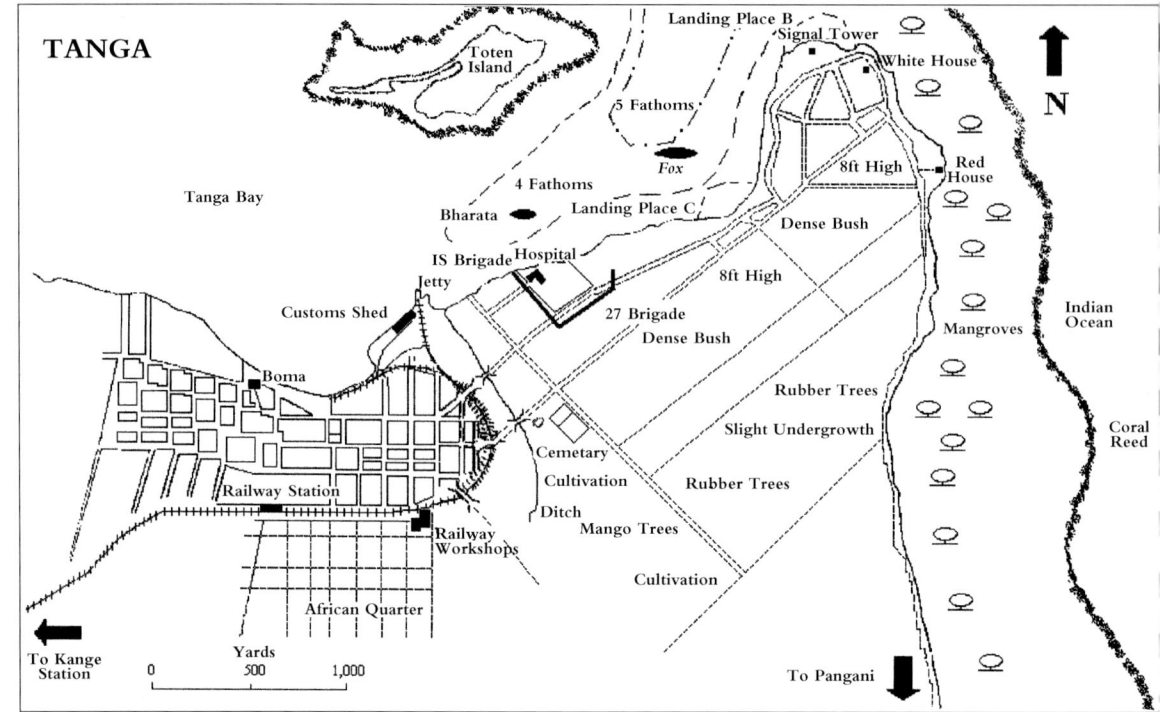

Map 13. The situation at 1800 hours, 4 November.

their efforts, particularly in officers, while the 2nd and 3rd Kashmir Rifles together with the 2nd Loyal North Lancashire were still capable of further effort. As well, half of the 13th Rajputs, and that battalion's and the 63rd's machine gun detachments, had performed well in battle.

In the end, despair won out and the GOC was convinced that another attack could lead to complete disaster, with the force being driven into the sea. These gloomy prognostications caused Aitken to drop the plan and begin considering the alternatives. IEF B had lost its collective confidence; Maj. King believed that both Aitken and his chief of staff, Col. Sheppard, had been hit hard by the defeat of the preceding day.[2] If the commander had lost his will to win, then there was little chance of inspiring the troops to a final effort.

Having ruled out another attack on Tanga, Aitken now had to consider his remaining options. The first was to consolidate at the Ras Kasone beachhead and regroup his force for a later attempt. While tempting, this had the drawbacks of insufficient water and being forced to re-organise his troops in a small and densely vegetated area in close proximity to the opposition. Given the state of the force, this process might take some time, and the Germans could well concentrate their forces for a major blow that would drive the British into the sea. Without the prospect of an early success, this course of action had little to recommend it.

The second choice was that of complete evacuation. This meant the abandonment of the strategic initiative and the admission of defeat. While unpalatable, it did offer the chance to bring off the force and return to British East Africa where it could refit itself in safety. On the other hand, it was potentially very risky, as German counter-attacks were expected and there were large numbers of seriously wounded cases to evacuate together with considerable quantities of stores, weapons and ammunition. Furthermore, the large number of Indian and African labourers which had just been landed would have to be re-embarked, potentially under fire. They had already demonstrated their propensity to panic at the first sound of gunfire and could easily disrupt the withdrawal. Finally, re-embarkation onto the transports was fraught with risks as the troops would be extremely vulnerable as they waited on the beaches to board the lighters. However, there seemed no workable alternative and Aitken made the fateful and difficult decision to evacuate.[3]

The forward troops were still within 1,000 yards of Tanga, occupying hasty defensive positions. At 2000 hours, the senior military and naval commanders met to discuss the plan for the morrow. With over 300 wounded, many of them seriously, and several thousand anxious agitated porters to organise, a night move was ruled out. This meant that Landing Places B and C, which could be observed from the town, were considered too vulnerable for use in daylight despite the presence of the *Fox* in the harbour. By default, Landing Place A, with its attendant coral reef and steep cliffs, became the sole evacuation beach. A considerable amount of detailed co-ordination took place while the weary and hungry troops dozed in their rudimentary trenches.[4]

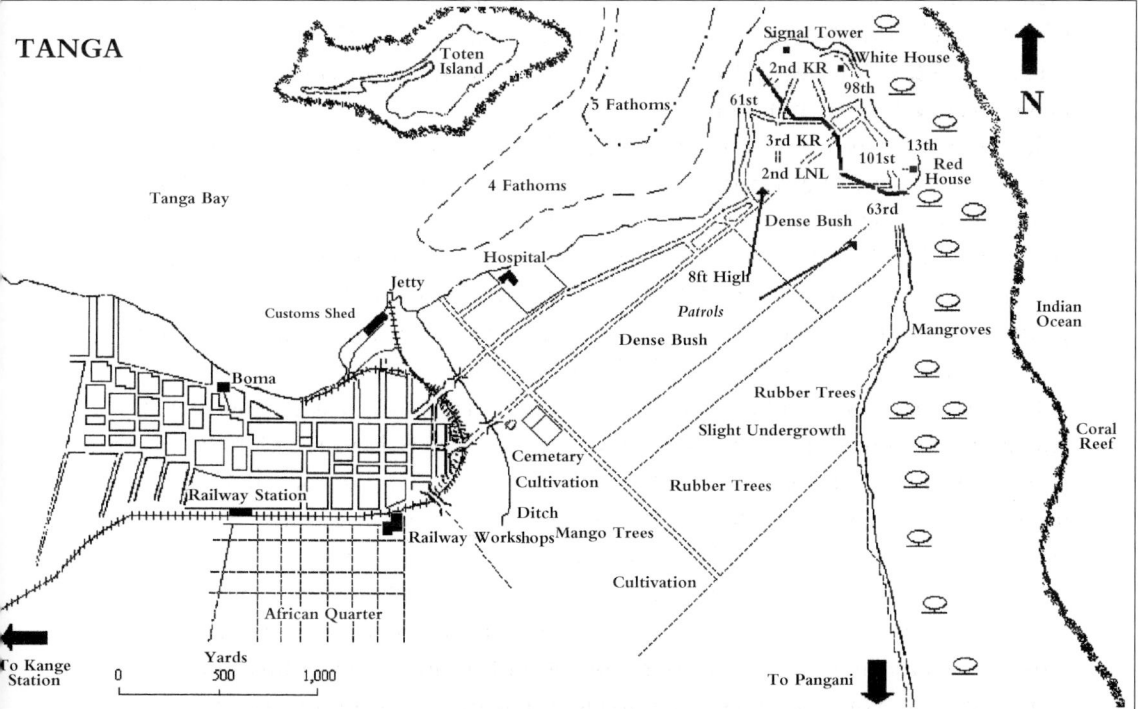

Map 14. The situation at 0100 hours, 5 November.

58. The 98th Infantry preparing defences.

The brigades were quietly pulled back during the night in order to form a solid perimeter around the now vulnerable beaches. The two best battalions, the North Lancashire and 2nd Kashmir Rifles, were given the task of holding the line under the orders of Gen. Tighe. Both units were reinforced by the machine guns of the remaining units and local patrols were placed forward of the trenches. The other units were corralled into rough order although large numbers of stragglers remained unaccounted for. By midnight, orders had been issued, the defences were fully manned and the tired troops managed some rest.

However, IEF B spent a very uncomfortable and jittery night of 4/5 November owing to the demoralisation of many and the expectation of a devastating German attack. Interestingly, stragglers from the Kashmir Rifles informed Aitken that the Germans had started digging trenches with great vigour around Tanga.[5] Without patrols of his own, Aitken was unable to verify these reports or assure himself that the enemy was not preparing for an attack. The situation was not helped by a number of alarmist reports that the Germans were massing for an attack. After some difficulty in rousing the exhausted troops, the force was stood to at 0500 hours, but nothing appeared. Morale was not helped by a violent thunderstorm half an hour later that half filled the trenches with water.[6]

The night passed quietly, with the first excitement coming near daybreak when a few shots were fired, causing a minor panic in the rear areas. A number of soldiers and labourers ran into the water seeking to escape and it was some time before order was restored. It was unclear whether the shots came from a German patrol or whether they were fired by a nervous sentry, but it was clear that the troops were extremely jittery.

However, the main problem was that of the prompt and efficient re-embarkation from Landing Place A. The importance of meeting the tides had been learnt on 3 November, as the coral reef still presented an obstacle to the heavier lighters. The solution was to wait for the flooding tide that was due at about 1300 hours before starting the evacuation. Ships' boats would be used to bring the troops off the beach to the lighters. They would have to transfer across and then the boats would have to return to pick up another party of men. This was a relatively simple operation, if slow and vulnerable. Much more controversially, there were concerns that heavy weights such as ammunition boxes and machine guns might hole the boats. This prompted the decision that all such items would have to be left behind.[7] Apart from the loss of such important material to the force, this ruling would leave everything to the enemy. No one seems to have asked the question as to how such vital weapons and munitions came to be safely landed in the first place or whether they could be taken off on larger vessels. Confidence had been lost and an attitude of *sauve qui peut* began to take hold.

This was compounded by the failure of the chain of command to take any official steps to destroy the vast quantities of ammunition being left behind, most of it still in its packing crates. Requests to break up the rounds and throw them into the sea were turned down, despite the ample time and lack of enemy pressure. Indeed, Col. Sheppard expressed the fear that there might be a panic and that the men would have to throw away their rifles.[8] Fortunately, some units disregarded the orders although only a small proportion of ammunition was dumped in deep water. However, for the most part, medical panniers, signalling equipment and personal kit bags were all left abandoned.[9]

While these machinations were underway, Lettow was recovering from the blunder of the day before. His equally exhausted troops marched through the night to reoccupy their abandoned positions and consolidate their hold on Tanga. However, these moves had precluded a follow-up of the British force and there was no contact apart from the odd patrol. As day broke and further reserves arrived at Kange Station, the German commander felt confident enough to press forward. More substantial firepower in the form of two obsolete C73 field guns had arrived during the night and they were brought forward into the town.[10]

By 0700 the guns began to engage the three ships in the harbour, with the transport *Laisang* being hit a number of times. That ship weighed anchor and departed, leaving only the *Bharata* and *Fox* in the inner harbour. The mountain guns on the former were unable to engage owing to the ship's swinging in the tide, but the light cruiser was able to check the enemy fire with several rounds from its 6-in. guns.[11] A violent rain shower forced a pause in battle, whereupon the Germans resumed their sniping and firing at the *Fox*, as the *Bharata* had departed for re-

59. The Red House, used as a hospital. The most seriously wounded casualties were left here with their doctors for capture.

embarkation duties. Capt. Caulfeild brought his ship in close to the jetty where it remained under sniper fire although little damage was done. At 1100 hours, the field guns resumed firing, but were quickly silenced by the ship's main armament.

As this minor naval engagement was taking place in the inner harbour, events at Ras Kasone were continuing. A number of stragglers turned up through the night while the paths down the cliffs were improved. 130 of the most seriously wounded cases were collected together at the field hospital located at the Red House as they were deemed incapable of movement. Along with five doctors, they were to be left there for capture.[12] Matters remained very tense, yet throughout the period there was no pressure from the Germans at all.

If the planning and execution of the original landings had been poor, the evacuation was much better organised. Some thirty ships' boats were sent out to the beaches while the lighters and tugs moved forward to the coral reef. The first lifts began at 1300 hours on the rising tide with the evacuation of the non-combatant Indian followers and African carriers. Shortly after proceedings had commenced, however, a German patrol reached the perimeter defences and fired a number of shots. Given the panicky mood, on hearing this large numbers of troops and followers bolted into the sea, swimming out to the boats and nearly swamping a

number of them. The patrol was driven off and order was only restored with difficulty. The re-embarkation then continued at full pace.[13]

As soon as the labour force had been brought off, the rearward units began to pull
back in the order 61st, 63rd, 98th, 101st and 13th Rajputs. Again the loss of confidence showed, as the need for haste was considered paramount, with the result that
the beach parties were instructed to load the troops without regard for unit integrity.
Boats were sent to the nearest ship regardless of affiliation which led to great
confusion and an enormous and unnecessary loss of equipment. Matters moved
quickly thereafter, fuelled by the desire to escape and much improved procedures. By
1500 hours only the covering force and the seriously wounded remained ashore.[14]

The final phases of the withdrawal were executed without difficulty as the 2nd
Kashmir Rifles embarked on the boats and were finally followed by the 2nd Loyal
North Lancashire at 1520 hours. Despite their worst fears, the evacuation had gone
smoothly and had been almost completely unhindered by German action.[15]
However, the decision to abandon the machine guns and ammunition was as
bitterly resented as it was seen as unnecessary.[16]

Once the force was re-embarked, the convoy did not leave immediately as the
problem of dealing with the many seriously wounded soldiers remained. During

60. The withdrawal on 5 November.

61. The withdrawal on 5 November. The mangrove swamps are particularly visible .

62. SS *Cupid* and lighters. The vessel is heavily overloaded while the differing sizes of the lighters can be seen.

the afternoon of 5 November, Capt. Meintertzhagen, a fluent German speaker, was ordered ashore to arrange a truce in order to deal with the casualties. He and Capt. von Hammerstein, Lettow's principal staff officer, came to an arrangement whereby a twenty-four hours' truce would prevail during which the British would be allowed to embark the wounded onto the ships. However, all such personnel were allowed off under parole with the proviso that they were not to serve again in the war.[17]

During his visit behind German lines, Meinertzhagen was able to glean a great deal of information about the morale and state of the German troops, both of which seemed high. Indeed, several of his opponents expressed the greatest admiration for the behaviour of the North Lancashires, with Hammerstein stating, 'Good troops will always face rifle fire but few troops will face machine gun fire at close quarters as your fellows did.'[18]

On a more negative note, during his visit the next day, the intelligence officer was informed that thirty unwounded sepoys had surrendered in the hospital that same morning, while during the battle of 4 November, another fifty had entered the hospital as malingerers. Conversely, the Germans let it be known that they considered their three battalions to be better than regular units in Germany and that it was no shame to have lost against such troops.[19]

Ironically, it was on receiving this request to evacuate casualties that Col. Lettow realised that Tanga was fully his and that he had won the battle. This cease-fire lasted until the afternoon of 6 November when they finally demanded that the

63. A last look at Tanga Harbour from SS *Nairung*.

British leave. A total of forty-nine wounded men were left behind in German hands as they were too unwell to be moved, even under the terms of the truce.

On the German side, news was only slowly emerging that victory was theirs. More reinforcements had arrived through the night with *9 FK* in Tanga and a further two and a half companies on the march. By morning, Lettow had twelve companies, comprising 310 Europeans, 1,220 *Askaris*, twenty-one machine guns and five guns; a formidable force. However, he admitted that he dared not follow up the British, although he made the statement that:

> It was not now advisable to advance with all our forces against the enemy, who was re-embarking at Ras-Kasone, as the country there was entirely open, and commanded by the cruisers lying in its immediate vicinity.[20]

The assertion about the country would have surprised most participants and it seems more likely that Lettow was unaware of the scale of his victory. Some of his troops were hardly trained and a number had broken during the assault the previous day. Furthermore, all were exhausted and had had very little to eat for the better part of two days. A situation report on 5 November mentioned the success of the counter-attack on the previous day, but added that although the Indians had been driven back to the beaches, they were being reinforced for a renewed attempt on the town. It was really on the request for a truce that signalled the end of the battle.[21]

All of 6 November was spent in evacuating the wounded and burying the dead with the convoy remaining close to Tanga. Work went on well into the night as it

64. Overloaded transports on the way to Mombasa.

65. Damage in Tanga: the Hotel Kaiserhof was the scene of some of the heaviest fighting.

66. A building damaged by gunfire.

67. Damage in Tanga: the customs shed by the jetty.

proved difficult to move the serious cases onto the boats before taking them out to the ships. Finally, the task completed, the British withdrew from land, leaving it under German control and returned to their vessels. The truce was now ended and threatened with further bombardment if they lingered any longer, the expedition sailed for Mombasa on 7 November. It arrived there the next day in a disorganised and dejected state to begin the task of unloading and complete reorganisation. It was a dismal ending to an operation that had completely failed to meet its objectives and resulted in 817 casualties as compared to the 145 suffered by the much smaller German force.

The losses were telling:[22]

Unit	Killed	Wounded	Missing	Total	Strength	Percentage
2nd Loyal NL	29	63	23	115	832	13.8
63rd PLI	12	37	36	85	762	11.2
98th Infantry	7	33	39	79	762	10.4
101st Grenadiers	184	31	7	222	762	29.1
13th Rajputs	52	44	–	96	766	12.5
2nd Kashmir	14	27	–	41	732	5.6
3rd Kashmir	3	16	2	21	379	5.5
3rd Gwalior	1	1	–	2	379	0.5
61st Pioneers	52	57	39	148	766	19.3
Staff & Support	5	1	2	8	174	4.6
Total	359	310	148	817	6314	12.9

68. Damage in Tanga: the African hospital damaged by naval gunfire during the battle.

Undeniably, the 101st had suffered extremely heavily with 24.1% of the battalion being killed, while the much maligned 61st Pioneers and 13th Rajputs each lost fifty-two dead. The Kashmiris escaped relatively lightly considering their experiences, while the Gwalior's low figures reflect their position out of battle.

On the other side, German losses were high, especially among officers and NCOs (von Prince had fallen at the head of his troops),[23]

	Killed	Wounded	Missing	Total
Officers	5	9	–	14
NCOs	11	15	1	27
Askaris	35	52	–	87
Carriers	13	4	–	17
Total	64	80	1	145 (128 troops)

The loss rates were 12.9% for the British and 11.6% for the Germans engaged in the fighting. They were surprisingly close given the scale of the British defeat and the relative proportions involved. In absolute numbers, the attackers lost 6.4 times the defenders' casualties, which roughly reflected their relative battle strength of 5.7 times British troops to Germans. Either way, both sides suffered heavily although of course the Germans retained the field of battle and British morale was shattered.[24]

Equally important were the arms and equipment left behind by the British: some eight machine guns, 455 rifles, over 500,000 rounds of ammunition, medical panniers, rations and boxes of equipment. It was a major boost to the *Schutztruppe*'s scarce resources and a testament to the loss of will by Aitken's force.[25]

The reverse destroyed any chance of an early completion of the occupation of German East Africa and put the British on the strategic defensive. More importantly, the defeat enabled the Germans to consolidate their forces and prepare for a campaign that would last another four years.

9

EPILOGUE

The ignominious failure at Tanga was a major setback for British ambitions in East Africa. Almost immediately after the news was received in London, Aitken was informed that no announcements of the battle were to taken place.[1] When the battered and dejected IEF B arrived at Mombasa on 8 November, it was in urgent need of reorganisation and refitting. However, British East Africa's perceived defence needs took priority and the best units were quickly sent off to reinforce IEF C and the Protectorate forces. The remainder were kept near the port and began the lengthy process of re-equipment and re-training; a great deal needed to be done. Aitken tried to have the worst units sent back to India in disgrace, but the viceroy refused as there were no replacements and he feared the effects of the news.[2]

The Admiralty's concerns for the destruction of the *Königsberg* remained unabated and Gen. Tighe was immediately sent to the Rufiji delta to assess the possibility of army assistance. As the German ship was hidden in a tangled river basin and surrounded by swamps and jungle, Tighe replied that one and a half good battalions would be required and even then it would be a hazardous, with the real possibility of failure. After the reverse at Tanga, there were not that many such troops available and with reinforcements not forthcoming, the enterprise was left in the Admiralty's hands.[3] It would not be until July 1915 that the trapped cruiser was ultimately engaged and destroyed.

Meeting soon after the reverse, the Offensive Sub-Committee considered returning to the attack, but the GOC's reports on the state of his infantry and their inability to provide additional reinforcements quickly put paid to this idea. With the British forces fully committed in France and elsewhere, Lord Kitchener ordered East Africa onto the defensive while taking over responsibility for operations himself.[4]

For the land forces, November was spent in a series of moves around the British colony with the aim of guarding the all-important Uganda railway. IEFs B and C were merged with the local forces and placed under Gen. Aitken's command. No longer capable of serious offensive operations, the force became focused on static defence with Tighe becoming commander of Mombasa district, while Wapshare took over Nairobi district. An uneasy stalemate followed with both sides holding a number of strong, fixed defences and sending out patrols to disrupt the other. This situation would last through most of 1915 and into early 1916 when a renewed British offensive was finally launched. However, the fighting in East Africa would not finish until after the main armistice in November 1918, and ended up in Northern Rhodesia.

For Gen. Aitken, the fiasco at Tanga weakened his position considerably. His explanation of the expedition to the Indian Secretary was not convincing and his report, that made wild and unsubstantiated claims that over 4,000 Germans, all of them gentlemen, had opposed him while reinforced by reservists from Australia and China, lost him further credibility.[5] Neither Lord Kitchener in the War Office nor the Commander-in-Chief, India, were impressed with the tone of Aitken's telegrams and the fact that he had not landed his guns. He was deemed unfit for independent command and on 4 December 1914, he was recalled to the United Kingdom.[6]

On return to London, Kitchener refused to see Aitken, and Gen. Barrow, the mastermind of the adventure, received him very coldly. This was to be the end of Aitken's career as he was never employed again, despite the pressures of the war, and lost his temporary rank, reverting to his permanent rank of colonel. Feeling unjustly treated, Aitken tried his best to get reinstated, writing to the Secretary of State for India in 1915. However, he was unsuccessful in attracting much support until after the war, when his case was reviewed by both the War and India Offices. Although there was no clear-cut document about his dismissal, Aitken was informed that he had most probably been removed for a long string of reasons:

a.   Acting without sufficient information
b.   Not landing first at Mombasa.
c.   Landing and size of Gen. Tighe's force.
d.   Want of proper reconnaissance.
e.   Not landing himself before 5 p.m.
f.   Not taking his brigadiers into his confidence.
g.   Commencing attack too late in the day.

Aitken was able to rebut most of these charges, and relied on the poor quality of the troops and the naval truce as mitigating factors.[7] By this time, he had convinced himself that others were at fault with the intelligence officers and lack of information being to blame. Furthermore, he now tried to blame Caulfeild's lack of urgency as a major reason for the failure:

> Capt. Caulfield [sic] was to summon the Governor of Tanga on board H.M.S. 'Fox', demand the surrender of Tanga unconditionally, and at the end of one hour after the arrival of the German Governor on board, we were to commence landing at once.[8]

Unfortunately, this subsequent assertion is nowhere supported in his own operation orders or war diary; indeed they stated that the time of disembarkation would depend on whether minesweeping operations were necessary or not. Aitken later went much further, stating:

> I have the honour to say, that the action taken by the S.N.O. in the opening phase of the Tanga operations was entirely, and in all respects, contrary to my intentions, and to the instructions he had received clearly from me… and my whole plan of operations was consequently seriously jeopardised at the best, and (as it turned out) entirely wrecked.[9]

This was entirely incorrect as Aitken was in possession of the naval orders from the evening of 31 October onward and there is no record of any dispute. Indeed the entry for 2 November clearly shows that this was expected:

> Convoy reached 1st rendezvous at daybreak, & FOX steamed into TANGA outer harbour, with orders from G.O.C. Force that nothing short of unconditional surrender would be accepted.[10]

There was no mention of a failure to fulfil orders and his own despatch, written a few days after the battle, stated that the *Fox* was to go in on its own. It seems likely that unable to consult official files and angry about his treatment, Aitken managed to convince himself that others had been at fault. While understandably keen to clear his own name, it was a rather unsavoury means of doing so.

After a lengthy correspondence, including with the Admiralty, which naturally disputed this view, the War Office wrapped up its investigation with a judgement. It concluded that the failure to hear his explanation and the refusal to employ him were unjust to Aitken while accepting that the abrogation of the truce and poor quality of the troops could not be held against him. Opinions were also swayed by Lettow's own account of the battle which emphasised the mobility and quality of his own force.[11] In this, they were being kind to Aitken as no mention of the quality of his generalship was made. Finally, by way of recompense, he was promoted to honorary brigadier general and given the maximum pension of a colonel.[12]

On the naval side, shortly after the landings, the Admiralty questioned Caulfeild about his role in the fiasco, particularly the truce.[13] He used the captain of the *Chatham*'s extraordinary justification that the shelling was against a ship and not the town: 'CHATHAM is of opinion that her shells [struck] steamer entirely and [were therefore] only part of KONIGSBERG operations and I concur in this view.' In Caulfeild's view this left the main truce intact.[14]

This was completely at odds with Drury-Lowe's statements made in Dar-es-Salaam harbour on 22 October and his own signals to the Admiralty. Frankly, such a distinction can only have existed in his own mind although it is more likely that he was trying to save a fellow captain from court-martial. As regards the slowness of the landings, Caulfeild countered with:

Had he [Aitken] at any time impressed on me the necessity of landing the whole force with utmost despatch or indeed betrayed by word or manner any time, on account of probable opposition, etc., despatch was of vital importance I should willingly have taken the responsibility of endeavouring to bring in all ships together.[15]

As it was, Churchill ordered Caulfeild to exchange ships and to return to the United Kingdom, no doubt to justify himself. However, the Sea Lords were less harsh and persuaded the First Lord to let Caulfeild retain command of the *Fox* and remain on station. Caulfeild went on to command an old battleship, and ended the war as a rear admiral.

Coming at the end of a long and bloody war, there seems to have been little appetite for an interservice dispute about an unfortunate battle that seemed best forgotten. Neither officer had distinguished themselves and both had shown questionable judgement. The War Office was reluctant to question Aitken's original dismissal and agreed that his subsequent treatment had been unfair. In the circumstances, it was perhaps the best solution.

For the Germans, Tanga was the successful start to what was to become a very long and hard-fought campaign. For Col. Lettow, it was a triumphant vindication of both his strategy and methods, while giving colonial morale a great boost. It established the *Schutztruppe*'s reputation as skilled and determined fighters who were not to be taken lightly. More importantly, it gave the Germans time to expand and further train their forces to a higher level.

Lettow went on to become the star of the entire campaign, respected by Germans and British alike. The Kaiser later awarded him the *Pour le Mérite*, Germany's highest honour, with subsequent promotion to *Generalmajor* for his efforts. He remained in command of the beleaguered *Schutztruppe* for the remainder of the war, leading his enemies through German East Africa and Portuguese East Africa before surrendering, on order, on 13 November 1918 in Northern Rhodesia. After the war he became a national hero and became a brigade commander in the new *Reichswehr*. However, his authoritarian sympathies could not be suppressed in the political ferment of the Weimar Republic and he was involved in the failed Kapp *Putsch* of 1920. This ended his army career as he was dismissed for his participation in the attempted *coup*.

Tanga had made the shortcomings in the British war machine glaringly obvious. Ominously, there was no sign of wishing to learn from the failure – that the inability to learn from mistakes was another defect would become clear during the Dardanelles of the following year.

10

CONCLUSIONS

Outwardly, the battle of Tanga was a major defeat for the British who had failed to use their overwhelming strength to capture a barely defended town before being beaten in battle by the more tactically nimble Germans. While this was true, the battle was in many ways a close run thing that could have been won by either side. Both sides made major errors, although the Germans made fewer mistakes and recovered much more quickly. From the British perspective, the best that can be said is that individual gallantry was let down by major failures at all the major levels of command. Gen. Aitken failed in his role of an independent commander although the blame for failure was far from being uniquely his.

The whole concept of the expedition was flawed almost from the outset. Initially, the concept of removing a coastal wireless station and the main port in the Indian Ocean was sound and relatively easy to achieve, although a detailed plan was never actually worked out. However, it was Gen. Barrow's plan for turning a raid into a full scale invasion that seriously unhinged matters. His grandiose ideas were taken at face value; neither the Admiralty nor the India Office subjected them to any sort of critical analysis and there is no evidence that a proper military appreciation was ever carried out. Certainly, the strategic value of German East Africa was low; its only worth would be as a pawn for any peace negotiations. This led to a completely inadequate force being sent on a risky and strategically dubious mission. By September 1914, it was clear that the Germans had a most formidable army and that it might be reasonable to assume that their colonial troops might be of a high standard too.

Some of the blame for the muddle must also fall on the various Whitehall departments. The operation was rightly the province of the War Office, which should have been in charge. In the exceptional circumstances, passing responsibility to the India Office was not unreasonable, provided that Army Headquarters, India, actually ran matters. However, the combination of Barrow's intervention, amateur strategy and wishful thinking allowed the aims of the project to spiral out of control. Furthermore, petty rivalries between the Colonial, India and War Offices prevented the military commanders from communicating effectively.

The Admiralty's handling of the truce deserves special consideration. It correctly realised the impossibility of maintaining local truces in a general war and rightly refused to ratify them. However, in trying to be too clever, they left the abrogation to the last minute and failed to consider the changed circumstances following the sinking of the *Pegasus* and *Chatham*'s subsequent visit to Dar-es-Salaam. Poor staff work and the bypassing of the local commander-in-chief meant that the naval operations surrounding the landings were muddled. This was aggravated by Churchill's relentless focus on the *Königsberg* and the lack of concern for the landings. Greater problems were only avoided by fortunate non-compliance with his orders. Similarly, the Admiralty and the India Office both failed to inform Gen. Aitken of the truce and it was left to Capt. Caulfeild to announce its existence just days prior to the landing.

It was the local handling of the naval truce that evoked the most outrage at the time. Despite its obvious importance, Caulfeild failed to clarify matters with either his commander-in-chief or the Admiralty. As SNO, he was well aware of planned operations as well as of the hunt for the *Königsberg*. His insistence on a formal abrogation on the morning of the landings may be criticised for over-zealousness, although he was following the letter of his instructions. The point is that he should have tried to find a workable solution while there was still time to do so.

If London set a poor example of planning, then Gen. Aitken seems to have amplified it. Despite having had several months in which to consider the possibilities of the attack, he does not appear to have come up with much before arriving at Mombasa. Apart from a dogged belief that the Germans would surrender at the first sight of the Indian Army, his plan was fatally compromised by its lack of clarity. It presupposed an unopposed entry into the town, making the landing of stores and staff baggage a greater priority than his second brigade. He anticipated meeting any resistance only once the force was ashore and the base developed. This credited the Germans with an extremely poor sense of initiative. Again, Aitken was well aware that IEF C would be available to support his landings, but he did nothing to alert Stewart about his intentions until the conference at Mombasa. Thereafter, it was given the vague task of 'co-operation' with its ultimate aim apparently of accepting the German surrender in the north.

However, early on 2 November, it was quite clear that the Germans were not going to surrender and therefore some resistance might be expected. Nevertheless, Aitken persisted in putting the 61st Pioneers ashore after the 13th Rajputs, as the former would be needed to build up the base facilities. He failed to consider a fight might occur and when it did, turning out unfavourably, he immediately landed the 2nd Loyal North Lancashire, thereby mixing up his brigades and wrecking the landing plan.

Poor planning was also reflected in the inept manner in which the landings were carried out. The failure to have a contingency plan of any sort was inexcusable, as was the failure to reconnoitre an alternative landing place beforehand. The delays in returning to the convoy and then of convening a conference meant that 2 November was a wasted day. That there was no sense of urgency was clear from both the naval disembarkation instructions and the order of landing. Neither

Aitken nor Caulfeild seemed unduly concerned about conducting amphibious landings against a hostile shore.

These initial flaws were compounded by Caulfeild's decision to bring forward only three transports during the night of the 2/3 November. Apart from the fact that the Imperial Service Brigade was split up, a lack of rehearsal and training meant that loading was slow and painful. By not starting until darkness had fallen, further delays were almost unavoidable. However, it was the launching of the lighters at a known time of low tide and their subsequent grounding on the coral reef that was an elementary mistake for a senior naval officer. Furthermore, despite his later protestations, his lamentable slowness of landing the force on an enemy shore after three months of war was deplorable. It took over thirteen hours from the time that the ultimatum was due until the first troops were even ready to land, and seventeen hours before the first battalion was ashore. To make matters worse, after the setback on 3 November, Aitken declined to hasten the arrival of 27 Brigade during the next night as he feared a German attack. The end result was that it took over forty-eight hours to land the bulk of his combat troops. In the end, the loss of surprise and time incurred through the breaking of the truce would not have been fatal in themselves had there been a sound plan and vigorous execution of the landings thereafter.

The GOC paid little attention to the preparation of his force, although in fairness his time was quite limited. However, the troops had spent at least two weeks in cramped and unpleasant conditions on board ship in a tropical climate. Consequently, their physical fitness had deteriorated and many had suffered from sea-sickness. Apart from a few days for the Imperial Service Brigade, they had had no opportunity to train together in India and none were experienced in amphibious operations. The majority had been equipped with new rifles and machine guns just before embarking, making individual proficiency difficult. Finally, he lacked confidence in several of his battalions, but nevertheless gave them important roles.

On the ground, the sketchiness of Gen. Aitken's planning did little to help. However, Gen. Tighe did press on as quickly as he could with his limited forces. Following the failure of the first attempt to take the town, Aitken then tolerated a lengthy and deliberate build-up at a time when he knew that the Germans were re-deploying down the Usambara Railway. The failure to use his sound troops for patrolling or probes on the nights of the 3/4 or 4/5 November was remarkable and he missed both chances to occupy the empty town.

Lack of firepower was one of the biggest weaknesses to the British order of battle. It had been blithely assumed that a single battery of mountain guns would provide sufficient fire support to capture German East Africa. Aitken's decision to leave his guns on board ship during the second attack was a disastrous one, especially after the limitations of this deployment had been shown on 3 November. Although the terrain was close, mountain guns were used to firing in the direct role and could have been employed in the close support of the infantry and suppressing the very effective German machine guns. The failure to provide an effective system of communication or pre-arranged signals meant that the best that could be achieved was random fire into the seafront. This same shortcoming reduced the powerful guns on the *Fox* to ineffectiveness.

After the battle, a great deal of blame was heaped on the very poor performance of some of the Indian Army units. It is clear that that the 63rd Light Infantry collapsed under relatively slight pressure as did the 61st Pioneers on the second day, while the 98th Infantry plus elements of the 13th Rajputs refused to advance against the enemy. The 3rd Gwaliors were virtually useless throughout and ultimately deemed unfit to serve as guard forces. These bad showings were offset by the fine behaviour of the 2nd and 3rd Kashmir Rifles, the 101st Grenadiers and part of the 13th Rajputs. These battalions fought some determined actions and suffered a large number of casualties. It was easy to blame the soldiers for running away, but little thought was directed at the system that allowed for such badly trained units to exist as well as their lack of real preparation for war. Apart from some limited small arms firing before departure, there had been no training for fighting in bush conditions, no rehearsals of boat work and landings or brigade operations. In the circumstances, it was far from surprising that individual fitness and morale was not good.

Intelligence was an area in which both sides did reasonably well. Aitken later claimed to have had virtually no information about Tanga, but this seems not to have been the case. Norman King wrote a very useful and accurate guide on the enemy colony while two local planters, one of whom had lived in the town, were attached to the headquarters. Furthermore, Gen. Tighe and a number of officers had served in East Africa previously and were familiar with the problems of bush fighting in a hot climate. Aitken made little use of this knowledge and dismissed the support of the KAR outright. British intelligence about the dispositions and re-deployment times of the *Schutztruppe* were quite accurate, yet nothing in the planning or orders indicated their potential speed of response or fighting power.

It is also notable that despite the long build up period, he did not press either the troops already in British East Africa or the Royal Navy for further information about the nature of the ground. The paucity of detailed information about Tanga did not preclude the cover reconnaissance of potential beaches by agents or intelligence officers yet virtually nothing was done beforehand.

The Germans while justly reckoning on Tanga as a major victory, were not free from problems themselves, and nearly lost the battle on two occasions. The initial dispositions were hindered by the intensifying conflict between the governor and his *Kommandeur*. This was to result in confusion over the implementation of the truce as Lettow sought to repel any landings while Schnee wished to avoid damage to the towns. It also led to both Tanga and Dar-es-Salaam being virtually undefended at a time when intelligence indicated that landings were imminent. It also led to schisms within the settler community with many unconvinced of Lettow's strategy.

Equally, it is hard to understand his dispositions given his apparent concern for the security of the ports. He had visited Tanga only several days prior yet he left just a tiny garrison of raw troops for its defence. Schnee had forbidden him to defend the town, but had agreed to defences around it and that it could be used for accommodation purposes. Instead of maintaining a sizeable garrison within easy range, such as at Kange or another plantation station, Lettow chose to keep the bulk of the trained troops in the Kilimanjaro area. This may have facilitated training and kept that area secure, but it left the port wide open to attack. As it was, two of Baumstark's three companies were up country near the border while elements of the third were moving to join them. The remainder of the *Schutztruppe's* main body were at least fifteen hours away and dependent on a single-track railway line. Against any competent foe, the town was virtually open to easy seizure. Lettow regarded Kilimanjaro as key to his defence plans, but given the known British forces in that area, a sustained offensive was hardly likely. He seems to have under-estimated the potential of sea power and his plan for defending Tanga can hardly be described as credible. He was indeed fortunate that his opponents managed to bungle matters so thoroughly.

Baumstark appears to have been an indecisive and unconfident commander. Instead of marching straight to the aid of *17 FK*, he halted *16 FK* at Kange where he sent a downbeat telegram to Lettow. Urged on, he then compounded matters by ordering the evacuation of the town just as the initial British thrust had been blunted. Then again on the afternoon of 4 November, he made the same decision, this time after the main enemy attack had been repulsed. He did not follow up closely enough and allowed the British to withdraw unscathed before leaving Tanga empty one more time.

Lettow had arrived early on 4 November and rapidly imposed his personality on the battle. After stiffening the resolve of the defenders, he fought an excellent defensive battle, committing his reserves at the decisive moment. Thereafter, he seems to have lost control as first the counter-attacking force lost momentum in the dense bush and second as he missed the withdrawal order issued by Baumstark. It took a number of hours to turn the force around and re-occupy the deserted town. Intriguingly, although he later blamed Baumstark for not immediately re-establishing contact with the enemy, Lettow failed to ensure that adequate patrols were sent to locate their positions. With IEF B in battered shape, it was extremely vulnerable to a sudden attack, yet Lettow considered the initial battle lost and was preparing to fight further inland. It was not until Meinertzhagen's arrival and request for a truce that he realised he had won.

Losses of irreplaceable German officers and NCOs were particularly heavy. On the whole the troops fought well, although Lettow noted a number of deficiencies in the training and discipline of the new troops. The failure to provide rations for the troops was a noted oversight and contributed greatly to their willingness to fall back so easily. He deplored their unavoidable reliance on the black powder rifles that produced the tell-tale clouds of thick smoke on firing. Finally, Baumstark came in for heavy criticism for lack of initiative.

In the final analysis, Gen. Aitken failed to provide the leadership, drive and judgement required of him. He was not up to the task, wildly over-ambitious as it was, while the Indian Army showed itself to be unprepared for modern war in terms of command, equipment, training and readiness. Similarly, the British peacetime system of planning and controlling world-wide military operations was unable to cope with the strains of general war. Although a general and naval war staff existed, at this stage in the conflict they were unable to function as they were intended, that is to provide considered, objective and realistic advice to civilian policy makers. Finally, the fiasco showed that there was no central apparatus for ensuring the close co-operation between the army and navy in joint operations. This defect was to re-emerge less than three months later during the preparations for the Dardanelles campaign. Tanga was a warning that was to be ignored at great cost in men, money and material.

Col. Lettow began the battle with faulty dispositions that should have cost him victory. Fortunately for him, his opponent squandered every opportunity presented and this enabled the German to recover his poise. Thereafter, he conducted the battle in a vigorous and determined manner, while his troops proved themselves to be fitter, better trained and better motivated than their counterparts. At Tanga, they won a major tactical and operational victory as the British invasion had been bloodily repulsed and they had to maintain substantial forces in East Africa in order to contain any possible threats to their own protectorate.

ANNEXE A
BRITISH ORDER OF BATTLE

INDIAN EXPEDITIONARY FORCE A

27th (Bangalore) Infantry Brigade	Troops	Followers	Total Strength
Brigade Headquarters	16	7	23
2nd Loyal North Lancashire Regiment	832	58	890
63rd Palamcottah Light Infantry	762	58	820
98th Infantry	762	58	820
101st Grenadiers	762	58	820
Brigade Signal Section	28	4	32
Total	3,162	243	3,405

Imperial Service Brigade

	Troops	Followers	Total Strength
Brigade Headquarters	5	5	10
13th Rajputs	766	58	824
2nd Kashmir Rifles	732	50	782
3rd Kashmir Rifles (1/2 battalion)	377	31	408
3rd Gwalior Rifles (1/2 battalion)	379	48	427
Brigade Signal Section	28	4	32
Total	2,287	196	2,483

Force Troops

	Troops	Followers	Total Strength
Force Headquarters	46	32	78
61st King George's Own Pioneers	766	52	818
28th Indian Mountain Battery	285	31	316
North-Western Railway Volunteers (gun detachment for armoured train)	4	5	9
Faridkot Sappers and Miners	165	23	188
25 Railway Company, Sappers and Miners 26 Railway Company, Sappers and Miners Railway Coolie Corps	776	716	1,492

No. 5 Pontoon Park (Bridging Train)	24	4	28
No. 3 Photo-Litho Section, Madras Sappers and Miners			
No. 4 Printing Section, Madras Sappers and Miners	12	6	18
Motor Cyclist Signal Section	10	–	10
Field Post Office	13	16	29
$\frac{1}{2}$ British Field Ambulance	13	34	47
$1\frac{1}{2}$ Indian Field Ambulance	39	54	93
Supply and Transport Personnel	22	–	22
Total	2,175	973	3,148

Lines of Communication Troops

Lines of Communication Headquarters	6	4	10
Section Headquarters	4	2	6
Two sections, Indian Clearing Hospital	13	23	36
No. 1 British Stationary Hospital	6	18	24
No. 2 Advanced Depot, Medical Stores	1	6	7
Field Post Office	4	6	10
Base Depot and Record Office	13	3	16
Base Ordnance Depot	11	48	59
No. 4 Engineer Field Park	18	19	37
$\frac{1}{2}$ Section, No. 3 British General Hospital	7	25	32
Three sections, No. 6 Indian General Hospital	39	67	106
X-Ray Section	2	5	7
No. 38 Sanitary Section	35	76	111
Field Disbursing Officer	11	2	13
Base Supply & Transport Depot	69	267	336
Supply Coolie Corps	10	511	521
Base Post Office	8	11	19
Total	257	1,093	1,350
Grand Total	7,881	2,505	10,386

Note:

Followers were civilians hired to support the military units. Their work ranged from the very menial to the clerical.

These totals do not include the many African porters raised at Zanzibar and Mombasa who accompanied the force.

ANNEXE B
GERMAN ORDER OF BATTLE

SCHUTZTRUPPE

II. Batallion (Coastal Area)	Date of Arrival
15 FK	5 Nov
16 FK	3 Nov
17 FK	2 Nov

Bahnhof Schutz (Railway)	
4 Sch K	3 Nov

Abteilung von Merensky (Neu Moschi)	
One platoon, 1 FK	3 Nov
6 FK	3 Nov
6 Sch K	3 Nov

Abteilung von Prince (Taveta)	
7 Sch K	3 Nov
8 Sch K	3 Nov

From Abteilung Kepler (Kilimanjaro)	
4 FK	4 Nov
13 FK	4 Nov
2. Batterie	5 Nov

Note:
At the end of 5 November 1914, the German total strength around Tanga had reached 310 Europeans, 1,220 Africans, twenty-one machine guns and five guns.

Notes and Bibliography

Chapter 1
Introduction

1. Travers, Tim, *Gallipoli 1915*, Stroud: Tempus, 2001, p.20. His comment about the planning for the Dardanelles was equally true for Tanga: 'They were, in effect, amateur strategists and tacticians. It was likely that whoever could first put together a plan that was generally agreeable would carry the day.'

2. Lettow-Vorbeck, Gen. Paul von, *My Reminiscences of East Africa*, London: Hurst and Blackett, 1920. Reprinted Nashville, Tennessee: The Battery Press, n.d. Henceforth, Lettow, *Reminiscences*.

3. Schnee, Dr Heinrich, *Deutsch-Ostafrika im Weltkrieg*, Leipzig: Quelle & Meyer, 1919.

4. Boell, Heinrich, *Die Operationen in Ostafrika*, Hamburg: Walter Dachert, 1951. Henceforth, Boell, *Die Operationen*.

5. CAB 45/7, 'Account of Tanga' by Lt-Col. Kirke, R.E. Kirke tried to publish an article in Army Quarterly, but was refused permission by the War Office.

6. Hordern, Lt-Col. Charles, *History of the Great War: Military Operations East Africa August 1914–September 1916*, London: HMSO, 1941. Reprinted Nashville, Tennessee: The Battery Press, 1990. Henceforth, Hordern, *Military Operations – East Africa*.

7. Meinertzhagen, Col. Richard, *Army Diary*, London: Oliver and Boyd, 1960.

8. Mosley, Leonard, *Duel for Kilimanjaro*, London: Weidenfeld & Nicolson, 1963; Gardner, Brian, *German East: the Story of the First World War in East Africa*. London: Cassell, 1967; Sibley, Maj. J.R., *Tanganyikan Guerrilla, Pan/Ballantyne Illustrated History of the First World War*, Book No. 4, London: Pan/Ballantyne, 1971; Miller, Charles, *Battle for the Bundu*, London: Macdonald and Janes, 1974. From reading Miller's account, it seems that he did not make extensive use of Boell's work.

9. Boyd, William, *An Ice-Cream War*, London: Hamish Hamilton, 1982.

10. Hoyt, E.P., *Guerrilla: Col. von Lettow-Vorbeck and Germany's East African Empire*, New York: Macmillan, 1981; James, Lawrence, *The Savage Wars: British Campaigns in Africa 1870–1920*, London: Hale, 1985; Farwell, Byron, *The Great War in Africa*, New York: W.W. Norton, 1986.

11. Strachan, Hew, *The First World War: To Arms*, Volume I, Oxford: Oxford University Press, 2001.

Chapter 2
The Strategic Situation in August 1914

1. Halpern, *Naval History*, London: UCL Press, 1994, pp.6–9 and 66–67.

2. Halpern, *Naval History*, pp.68–70.

3.   Corbett, *History of the Great War: Naval Operations*, I, London: Longmans, Green and Co., pp.151–153.

4.   Hordern, *Military Operations – East Africa*, p.7.

5.   Kaponen, *Development for Exploitation, German Colonial Policies in Mainland Tanzania 1884–1914*, Studia Historica 49, Helsinki: Finnish Historical Society, 1995, pp.306 and 310–311. In 1914, the colony's income was about 20 million marks while it was granted over 36 million marks in loans.

6.   ADM 123/137, 30 Jul '14, Telegram, *Hyacinth* to *Astraea* and *Pegasus*.

7.   King-Hall, *Naval Traditions and Memories*, London, 1926, pp.243–244.

8.   Schnee, *Deutsch-Ostafrika im Weltkrieg*, pp.25–27; Raeder, *Kreuzerkreig*, II, pp.125–126.

9.   Methner, *Unter drei Gouverneuren: 16 Jahre Dienst in den deutschen Tropen*, Breslau: Korn, 1938, pp.342–343; Raeder, Kapitän zur See E, *Der Krieg zur See 1914–1918, Der Kreuzerkrieg in den ausländischen Gewässern*, II, Berlin: E.S. Mittler & Sohn, 1923, pp.125–126.

10.   Raeder, Kapitän zur See E, *Der Krieg zur See 1914–1918, Der Kreuzerkrieg in den ausländischen Gewässern*, I, Berlin: E.S. Mittler & Sohn, 1922, pp.11–14; Raeder, *Kreuzerkrieg*, II, pp.122–123.

11.   Raeder, *Kreuzerkrieg*, II, pp.132–136.

12.   Corbett, *Naval Operations*, I, pp.152–153.

13.   CAB 21/3, Joint Naval and Military Committee for the Consideration of Combined Operations in Foreign Territory, 5 Aug '14. For brevity, it was usually called 'The Offensive Sub-Committee'. Henceforth, *Proceedings*.

14.   CAB 21/3, *Proceedings*, 5 Aug '14.

15.   CAB 21/3, *Proceedings*, 6 Aug '14.

16   Churchill, *The World Crisis*, I, London: Thomas Butterworth Limited, 1923, pp.283–284; Oxford and Asquith, Earl of, *Memories and Reflections*, II, London: Cassell and Company, 1928, p.25.

17.   CAB 21/3. There is a short two-page note entitled 'Naval Note on Joint Expedition to Dar Es Salaam', undated and unsigned attached to the proceedings of the meeting of 6 August. It was passed to the India Office for information. It hardly constitutes detailed or considered operational planning. Nothing from the military side can be found.

18.   Robertson, *Soldiers and Statesmen 1914–1918*, I, London: Cassell and Co., 1926, pp.158–159.

19.   Hankey, Lord, *The Supreme Command*, I, London: George Allen and Unwin, 1961, p.168. French, David, *British Strategy and War Aims*, pp.27–28; Corbett, *Naval Operations*, I, pp.128–129.

20.   CAB 21/3, *Proceedings*, 14 Aug '14, '…no formal proclamation annexing any such territory should be issued without specific instructions from His Majesty's Government, and further, that an agreement should be come to with our Allies to act on similar lines.'; French, *British Strategy*, p.15.

21.   Churchill, *The World Crisis*, I, p.283.

22.   MS Harcourt, dep 507, *Colonial Office Telegrams Circulated to the Cabinet August 1914–August 1915*; 22 Sep '14, Telegram No. 1, Secretary of State for the Colonies to the High Commissioner for South Africa; 3 Oct '14, Telegram No. 3, Secretary of State for the Colonies to the Governor East African Protectorate (for the Belgians); dep 507, 27 Aug '14, Telegram, No. 2, Secretary of State for the Colonies to High Commissioner for South Africa; and dep 590 *Foreign Office Print*, 26 Aug '14, Telegram No. 176, Sir Edward Grey to Mr

Carnegie (for the Portuguese); CAB 21/3, 12 Aug '14, Telegram Foreign Office to Sir F. Bertie; and Andrew, Christopher and Kanya-Forster, *France Abroad*, London: Thames and Hudson, 1981, pp.62–63 (for the French).

23.   French, *British Strategy*, pp.27–28; Strachan, *The First World War*, I, pp.505, 521 and 545–546.

24.   Fischer, *Germany's War Aim Aims in the First World War*, London: Chatto & Windus, 1967, pp.38–39; French, *British Strategy*, p.9–10 and 14; Langhorne, Richard. 'Anglo-German Negotiations Concerning the Future of the Portuguese Colonies 1911–1914', *Historical Journal*, XVI, No. 24, (1973), pp.378–379; Vincent-Smith, John, 'Britain, Portugal and the First World War', *European Studies Review*, 4, No. 3 (1974), pp.207–238; Vincent-Smith, J.D., 'The Portuguese Republic and Britain, 1910–14', *Journal of Contemporary History*, 10, No. 4 (1975), pp.707–727; Stone, Glyn, 'The Official British Attitude to the Anglo-Portuguese Alliance, 1910–45', *Journal of Contemporary History*, 10, No. 4 (1975), pp.729–741.

25.   Andrew and Kanya-Forster, *France Abroad*, p.57; Ritter, Gerhard, *The Sword and the Sceptre: The Problem of Militarism in Germany, III, The Tragedy of Statesmanship – Bethmann Hollweg as War Chancellor (1914–1917)*, translated by Heinz Norden, London: Allen Lane, 1973, pp.27–28.

26.   Fischer, Fritz, *Germany's War Aim*, pp.102–103; Mombauer, Annika, *Helmuth von Moltke and the Origins of the First World War*, Cambridge: Cambridge University Press, 2001, pp.235–237.

27.   Wack, Henry Wellington, *The Story of the Congo Free State*, New York: Putnam, 1905, pp.530–544.

28.   Schnee, *Deutsche Ostafrika*, pp.37–38; Hordern, *Military Operations – East Africa*, pp.527–528; CAB 8/5, Colonial Defence Committee, No. 431 M, 'East and West African Protectorates' Position in the Event of War with a European Power', 24 Jan '11. The British had examined and ruled out a declaration of neutrality for its East African colonies as early as 1911 as it saw neutrality favouring the Germans.

29.   Iliffe, John, *Africans: The History of a Continent*, Cambridge: Cambridge University Press, 1995, p.208; Monsun, Jamie, 'Relocating *Maji-Maji*', *Journal of African History*, 39, 1998, pp.115–120.

30.   Zirkel, Kirsten, 'Military Power in German Colonial Policy', *Guardians of Empire*, ed. Killingray, David and Omissi, David, Manchester: Manchester University Press, 1999, pp.97–98 and 101–104; Schnee, *Deutsch-Ostafrika im Weltkrieg*, pp.18–23 and 34–36; Lettow, *Reminiscences*, pp.20–22.

31.   Petter, Wolfgang, 'Das Offizierkorps der Deutschen Kolonialtruppen 1889–1918', *Das Deutsche Offizerkorps 1860–1960*, ed. Franz, Günther, Boppard am Rhein: Harald Boldt Verlag, 1977, pp.164–165.

32.   Lettow, *Mein Leben*, Biberach an der Riss: Koehlers, 1957, pp.112–115.

33.   BA/MA, N14/14, Boell papers, *Denkschrift über Mobilmachungsvorarbeiten für den Fall eines Krieges mit Grossmacht für Deutsch-Ostafrika*, 27 Apr '12.

34.   Lettow, *Reminiscences*, pp.18–19.

35.   BA/MA, N103/36, von Lettow-Vorbeck Papers, *Lettow Kriegtagesbuch*, Aug '14. Lettow kept a series of pocket books throughout the war that effectively acted as his personal war diary. Henceforth, *Lettow, KTB*.

36.   Petter, 'Deutsche Kolonialtruppen', pp.168–169; WO 157/1112, Intelligence Summary IEF B, 16 Oct '14.

37.   Schnee, *Deutsche-Ostafrika im Weltkrieg*, pp.58–60; IWM, 49538, *Schutztruppe Kriegstagebuch*, 5,

8 and 23 Aug '14. Henceforth, *Schutztruppe KTB*.

38. Lettow, *Reminiscences*, pp.27–28.

39. Mombauer, *Moltke*, pp.95–96, 139 and 205.

40. Hordern, *Military Operations – East Africa*, pp.559–561.

41. Moyse-Bartlett, *The King's African Rifles*, p.701.

42. Meinertzhagen, *Army Diary*, pp.86 and 103.

43. Boell, *Die Operationen*, p.30.

44. Hordern, *Military Operations – East Africa*, p.15; Moyse-Bartlett, *The King's African Rifles*, pp.260–264.

45. Boell, *Die Operationen*, p.29.

46. Boell, *Die Operationen*, p.29.

47. Lettow, *Mein Leben*, pp.120–121.

48. *Kreuzerkrieg*, II, pp.132–134. The *Landsturm* was comprised of older men who had already completed their military service.

49. Boell, *Die Operationen*, pp.28–29.

Chapter 3
The Decision to Despatch Indian Expeditionary Forces B and C

1. CAB 21/3, 'Joint Naval and Military Committee (Offensive Sub-Committee), Part 7 – East Africa', 7 and 17 Aug 1914.

2. Hordern, *Military Operations – East Africa*, pp.30–31.

3. CAB 21/3, 'Joint Naval and Military Committee (Offensive Sub-Committee), Part 7 – East Africa', 9 and 10 Aug 1914.

4. CAB 21/3, 'Joint Naval and Military Committee (Offensive Sub-Committee), Part 7 – East Africa', 17 Aug 1914.

5. IWM, PP/MCR/150, King papers, Diary 25, 26, 30 Aug and 1 Sep 1914; Hordern, *Military Operations – East Africa*, pp.60–62; IWM, 80/13/1, Aitken papers, 'Account of the Indian Expeditionary Force to German East Africa', pp.1–2. Henceforth, *Aitken Account*; CAB 21/3, 'Joint Naval and Military Committee (Offensive Sub-Committee), Part 7 – East Africa', 28 Aug 1914.

6. Hordern, *Military Operations – East Africa*, pp.62–63. The Imperial Service Brigade joined 27 (Bangalore) Brigade in Indian Expeditionary Force 'B'.

7. CAB 5/3, CID Paper 111-C, 'Expedition Against German East Africa', 18 Sep 1914, pp.1–2; CAB 21/3, *Proceedings*, 22 Sep 1914. Barrow's proposals were agreed at this meeting.

8. CAB 21/3, 'Joint Naval and Military Committee (Offensive Sub-Committee), Part 7 – East Africa, 5, 7 and 8 Sep 1914.

9. Hordern, *Military Operations – East Africa*, pp.66–67; CAB 5/3, CID Paper 112-C, 'Expedition Against German East Africa – Draft of Instructions Proposed for Issue to the GOC Expedition "B"', 28 Sep '14; CAB 21/3, *Proceedings*, 29 Sep 1914.

10. Hordern, *Military Operations – East Africa*, pp.51–52 and 530. The totals for the forces already landed only include those in relative proximity to the main German concentration.

11.   Corbett, *Naval Operations*, I, pp.280–281; Halpern, *Naval History*, pp.124–125; ADM 137/32, 5
       Sep '14, Memo Churchill to 1st Sea Lord; 30 Sep '14, Telegram H1219, Viceroy to War Office
       and Admiralty.

12.   Wynne, *Ambush*, London: Hutchinson and Co., 1937, p.27.

13.   Wynne, *Ambush*, pp.21 and 24–25; IWM, Johnson Papers, 77/109/1, 'Notes on the Account
       of the Action at Tanga by Maj.-Gen. Sir E.C.W. Mackenzie', pp.2–3. These notes were
       compiled many years after the battle; Meinterzhagen, *Army Diary*, p.109.

14.   Wynne, *Ambush*, pp.46–47; IWM 77/109/1, Johnson papers, 'Notes on the Account of the
       Action at Tanga', p.2; Meinterzhagen, *Army Diary*, pp.123 and 158–159; *India Army List*,
       Calcutta: Government of India, April 1906, April 1913 and October 1914.

15.   *India Army List*, Calcutta: Government of India, April 1913 and October 1914; IWM, 88/6/1,
       Wapshare papers, Diary for 1914; and *The Times*, 24 Dec '32, Obituary for Lt-Gen. Sir
       Richard Wapshare.

16.   *India Army List*, Calcutta: Government of India, April 1913 and October 1914; IWM 88/6/1,
       Wapshare papers, Eastbourne newspaper cutting 'Major-General M.J. Tighe – Eastbourne
       Resident to command in East Africa, *c*.1915.

17.   WO 95/5344, War Diary 61st Pioneers, 22, 29 Sep and 7, 8 Oct '14.

18.   WO 95/5318, War Diary 13th Rajputs, 11, 27, 29 Sep and 7, 8 Oct '14; Hordern, *Military
       Operations – East Africa*, p.70.

19.   Singh, Maj. K. Brahma, *History of Jammu and Kashmir Rifles 1820–1956*, New Delhi: Lancer
       International, 1990, pp.108–111.

20.   Hordern, *Military Operations – East Africa*, pp.68–69.

21.   Raeder, *Kreuzerkrieg*, II, pp.85 and 209. SMS *Emden* sank some sixteen merchant ships in
       September–October 1914, while *Königsberg* sank only one merchant ship, but destroyed one
       British light cruiser in the same period; ADM 137/14, 4 Nov '14, Note 1st Lord to Chief of
       Staff; 5 Nov '14, Telegram Admiralty to Senior Naval Officer, Mombasa. Both these commu-
       nications make Churchill's greater concern for trapping the *Königsberg* apparent.

22.   Hordern, *Military Operations – East Africa*, p.37.

23.   Moyse-Bartlett, *The King's African Rifles*, pp.266–267.

24.   Hordern, *Military Operations –East Africa*, pp.51–52.

25.   Hordern, *Military Operations – East Africa*, p.47.

26.   Lettow, *Mein Leben*, pp.9–15, 30–36, 46–115.

27.   Boell, *Die Operationen*, p.54.

28.   Hordern, *Military Operations – East Africa*, pp.51–52.

29.   Hordern, *Military Operations – East Africa*, pp.46–47.

30.   Boell, *Die Operationen*, p.56.

31.   Boell, *Die Operationen*, p.77. A common German designation was the *Abteilung* (detachment)
       that took the senior officer's name. It was usually abbreviated to *Abt*.

CHAPTER 4

LOCAL NAVAL OPERATIONS AND THE ILL-FATED TRUCE

1.   Hordern, *Military Operations – East Africa*, pp.12–13 and 77–85, Sketches 9–11.

2.   Boell, *Die Operationen*, p.75; Lettow, *Reminiscences*, p.22.

3.   ADM 137/9, 12 Aug '14, Telegram 104, Britannia, Simonstown to Admiralty.

4.   ADM 137/9, 18 Aug '14, Telegram 119, C-in-C Cape to Admiralty. The terms of the truce echoed those agreed at Dar-es-Salaam and specified that a maximum of fifty armed native police could be retained in the town.

5.   ADM 137/9, 17 Aug '14, Telegram 116, C-in-C Cape to Admiralty; 17 Aug '14, Telegram 102, Admiralty to C-in-C Cape.

6.   ADM 137/9, 26 Aug '14, Telegram 128, Admiralty to C-in-C Cape.

7.   ADM 137/9, 27 Aug '14, Telegram 156, C-in-C Cape to Admiralty.

8.   ADM 137/9, 30 Aug '14, Telegram, Admiralty to SNO Zanzibar.

9.   ADM 137/10, 19 Aug '14, Letter, Colonial Office to Admiralty.

10.   ADM 137/10, 26 Aug '14, Letter, Admiralty to Colonial Office. Copies of the relevant telegrams were included with the letter.

11.   ADM 137/10, 27 Aug '14, Telegram 156, C-in-C Cape to Admiralty.

12.   ADM 137/9, 27 Aug '14, Telegram 184, Admiralty to C-in-C Cape; the ships were the *Chatham*, *Weymouth* and *Dartmouth*.

13.   ADM 137/9, 1 Oct '14, Telegram 199, Admiralty to C-in-C East Indies.

14.   Keble Chatterton, *The Königsberg Adventure*, London: Hurst and Blackett, 1936, pp.54–56

15.   Boell, *Die Operationen*, pp.73–74; ADM 137/32, 23 Oct '14, Telegram *Chatham*, Mombasa to C-in-C East Indies, Admiralty and C-in-C Cape. ADM 123/139, *c.* early September, but received by the *Chatham* on 22 Oct '14. Note from C-in-C Cape to Resident, Zanzibar 'Home Government will not ratify terms of truce imposed on Dar-es-Salaam and Tanga. A notification to this effect should be conveyed to the respective Governors shortly before any further hostile act is committed against these places.'

16.   IWM, PP/MCR/150, King papers, Diary, 22 Oct '14.

17.   Boell, *Die Operationen*, pp.72–74.

18.   ADM 137/32, 23 Oct '14, Telegram 296, *Chatham*, Mombasa to Admiralty, C-in-C East Indies and C-in-C Cape Stations.

19.   IWM PP/MCR/150, King papers, Diary, 26 Oct '14.

20.   ADM 123/139, *c.* early September, but received by the *Chatham* on 22 Oct '14, Note from C-in-C Cape to Resident, Zanzibar 'Home Government will not ratify terms of truce imposed on Dar-es-Salam and Tanga. A notification to this effect should be conveyed to the respective governors shortly before any further hostile act is committed against these places.'

21.   Corbett, *Naval Operations*, I, p.377.

22.   WO 138/41 Aitken Personal File, 28 Aug '20, Letter Admiralty to War Office, enclosing statement by Rear Admiral Caulfield [*sic*], p.1.

23.   WO 157/1112, Intelligence Summary IEF B, 29 Oct '14. This contemporaneous document directly contradicts Hordern, *Military Operations – East Africa*, p.73 and Anderson, Ross, 'The Battle for Tanga, 2–5 November 1914', *War in History*, 8, (3), 2001, p.303. This means that

Aitken and his staff had about a day and a half to consider the truce prior to attending the Mombasa conference.

24. IWM, PP/MCR/150, King papers, Diary, 26 Oct '14.

25. CAB 45/6, 'Memorandum of the Operations at Tanga' to cover letter of 31 Jul '14 [*sic* – note attached to letter of 20 Feb '17]; PP/MCR/150, King papers, Diary, 9 Nov '14.

26. IWM, P80, Cooke papers, 'Field Notes on German East Africa, General Staff India, August 1914', p.65.

27. IWM, PP/MCR/150, King papers, Diary, 27, 29 and 31 Oct '14. Ishmael was described as being 'extremely clever, intelligent and capable and smart'. He claimed to be Persian, but a number of British considered him to be a Bombay Jew and he was forced to leave the Mombasa Club on account of racism. Given the prevailing sentiment of the time, his views would probably have not received much attention.

28. Russell, Maj. A., 'The Landing at Tanga, 1914', *Tanganyika Notes and Records*, No. 58, Mar/Sep 1962, p.103.

29. WO 157/1112, Intelligence Summary IEF B, 10 Oct '14.

30. WO 157/1112, Intelligence Summary, IEF B, 16 Oct '14.

31. Meinertzhagen, *Army Diary*, p.86.

32. CAB 45/6, 'Memorandum of the Operations at Tanga' to cover letter of 31 Jul 14 [*sic* – note attached to letter of 20 Feb '17], pp.4–7; Hordern, *Military Operations – East Africa*, pp.73–74. Col. Mackay and Maj. King had landed with the shore party from the *Chatham* and had conducted the negotiations with the German officials.

33. CAB 5/3, 28 Sep '14, CID Paper 112-C, 'Committee of Imperial Defence. Expedition Against German East Africa'. The crucial paragraph stated 'in so far as naval support may be necessary, you will act in close co-operation with the naval authorities, who will be instructed by the Admiralty to render you every possible assistance.'

34. Wynne, *Ambush*, p.52. Aitken's senior staff officer, Lt-Col. Sheppard, estimated that the Germans needed eighteen hours to make the rail journey from Moschi to Tanga. He was reasonably accurate.

35. ADM 137/10, 13 Aug '14, Telegram, Governor East Africa Protectorate to Secretary of State for the Colonies. This authorised the support of 500 King's African Rifles for the advance on German East Africa under IEF B.

36. ADM 137/32, 31 Oct '14, Telegram, Admiralty to C-in-C East Indies Station and Cape Stations. This signal ordered the *Fox* to help the *Chatham* blockade the *Königsberg* while the other two cruisers were sent after the *Emden*.

37. ADM 137/32, 30 Oct '14, Telegram, Zanzibar to Admiralty; 31 Oct '14, Telegram *Chatham* to Admiralty. This signal reported the *Königsberg* being some six miles up the mouth of the River Rufiji.

38. WO 95/5289, War Diary IEF B, 31 Oct '14.

39. WO 95/5289, War Diary IEF B, 31 Oct '14; War Diary IEF C, 31 Oct–2 Nov '14.

40. BA/MA, N14/1, Boell Papers, Kapitel 3, p.111.

41. BA/MA, N14/1, Boell Papers, Kapitel 3, 27 Oct '14, Telegram Governor to Headquarters, pp.112–113.

42. Wynne, *Ambush*, pp.18 and 26.

43. BA/MA, N14/1, Boell Papers, Kapitel 3, p.110.

44. BA/MA, N14/1, Boell Papers, Kapitel 3, p.111.

45. BA/MA, N14/1, Boell Papers, Kapitel 3, p.113.

46. CAB 11/117, 'Defence Plans for the Uganda and East Africa Protectorates, Revised to February 1912', p.4.

47. WO 95/5289, War Diary IEF C, 2 Nov '14.

48. Hordern, *Military Operations – East Africa*, pp.97–98; Boell, *Die Operationen*, pp.82–83.

CHAPTER 5
THE ULTIMATUM AND INITIAL LANDINGS

1. ADM 137/14, 1 Nov '14, Telegram *Goliath* to Admiralty; 4 Nov '14, *Goliath* to Admiralty. The condenser leaks necessitated losing steam for at least ten days and were subsequently in need of a dockyard refit.

2. WO 107/45, Letter Brig.-Gen. Malleson to Gen. Cowans, 21 Mar '15. In this private letter, Malleson stated that the captain of the *Goliath* asked for several days to effect repairs so as to take part in the landings. This was ignored.

3. Hordern, *Military Operations – East* Africa, p.70. The 63rd Palamcottah Light Infantry had embarked at Karachi on 30 Sep '14 with no subsequent opportunity to go ashore for training or fitness.

4. WO 95/5289, War Diary IEF B, 31 Oct '14, 'Naval Operations in Connection with the Passage of the Convoy to anchorage in Vicinity of Tanga Island, disembarkation of Troops, &c. dated 31st October 1914'.

5. Hordern, *East Africa*, 'Operation Order No. 1, dated 1 November 1914', p.534; WO 95/5289, War Diary IEF B, 31 Oct '14, 'Naval Operations in Connection with the Passage of the Convoy to anchorage in Vicinity of Tanga Island, disembarkation of Troops, &c. dated 31 October 1914'.

6. Hordern, *Military Operations – East Africa*, pp.534–535.

7. Hordern, *Military Operations – East Africa*, pp.534–541.

8. Hordern, *Military Operations – East Africa*, pp.536–541.

9. ADM 137/32, 5 Oct '14, Telegram 201, C-in-C East Indies to Admiralty; 13 Oct '14, Telegram 225, Admiralty to C-in-C East Indies. Churchill personally instructed the *Fox* to carry on with its 'special duties'.

10. ADM 137/32, 31 Oct '14, Telegram 259, Admiralty to SNO Mombasa.

11. ADM 137/32, 31 Oct '14, Telegram 259, Admiralty to SNO Mombasa and C-in-C East Indies.

12. ADM 53/42071, Log HMS *Fox*, 2 Nov '14. The *Fox* anchored in Tanga Harbour at 0705 hours.

13. Boell, *Die Operationen*, p.77. The convoy was first sighted at 0630 hours.

14. BA/MA, N103/96, von Lettow-Vorbeck papers, Buhl, 'Deutsche Ostafrika im Weltkrieg', pp.4–5. This claim was subsequently denied by Caulfeild. However, given the vehemence of the German response and the circumstances, it is plausible.

15. BA/MA, N103/96, von Lettow-Vorbeck papers, Buhl, 'Deutsche Ostafrika', p.5.

16. Boell, *Die Operationen*, p.77.

17. NAM, 6506/16, Priestland papers, [17 FK] *Gefechtbericht zum 2. und 3. November bei Tanga*, pp.1–2; BA/MA, N103/96, von Lettow-Vorbeck papers, Buhl, 'Deutsche Ostafrika', pp.5–6.

18. NAM, 6506/16, Priestland papers, *Gefechtbericht zum 2. und 3. November bei Tanga*, p.2.

19. Boell, *Die Operationen*, p.77.

20. WO 95/5289, War Diary IEF B, 2300 hours 2 Nov '14.

21. WO 95/5289, War Diary IEF B, 8 Nov '14, Sketch 2, Appendix 6.

22. ADM 53/42071, Log HMS *Fox*, 2 Nov '14. Caulfeild does not refer to the extended deadline for surrender, but his departure time is consistent with the German account; Wynne, *Ambush*, p.49.

23. Wynne, *Ambush*, pp.43–44.

24. IWM, PP/MCR/150, King papers, Diary, 1 Nov '14.

25. CAB 45/34, 2 May 33, Letter Cmdr Edward Headlam to Maj. Stacke. Cmdr Headlam was the Naval Transport Officer during the landings and considered Capt. Caulfeild's decision to be flawed. He believed that had the lead ship be given a pilot the rest would have followed willingly and promptly without undue danger. Unfortunately for the British, the SNO does not seem to have asked his advice during the landing period.

26. ADM 53/42071, Log HMS *Fox*, 2 Nov '14.

27. Schnee, *Deutsche-Ostafrika im Weltkrieg*, p.72; Boell, *Die Operationen*, p.78.

28. IWM, 92/18/1, Hammill papers, 'Lecture on Tanga'.

29. IWM, PP/MCR/150, King papers, Diary, 1–4 November 1914.

30. Hordern, *Military Operations – East Africa*, p.80; NAM, 6506/16, Priestland papers, *Gefechtbericht zum 2. und 3. November*, p.2.

31. WO 107/45, Letter Brig.-Gen. Malleson to Gen. Cowans, 21 Mar '15; WO 107/45, Letter Brig.-Gen. Malleson to General Staff, 'B' Force, 8 Nov '14, pp.2–3. Henceforth, *Malleson Report*.

32. WO 95/5318, War Diary 13th Rajputs, 2 and 3 Nov '14.

33. WO 158/439, 'Despatch on the Tanga Operations', p.4.

34. IWM, 88/61/1, Wapshare papers, Diary, 2 Nov '14.

35. Boell, pp.75 and 77; Hordern, *Military Operations – East Africa*, pp.103–104.

36. Boell, p.78; Hauer, August Dr, *Kumbake: Erlebnisse eines Artze in Deutsch-Ostafrika 1914–1919*, Berlin: Hobbing, 1922, p.56.

37. NAM, 6506/16, Priestland papers, *Gefechtbericht zum 2. und 3. November*, p.3.

Chapter 6

The First Attack – 3 November 1914

1. WO 95/5318, War Diary 13th Rajputs, 2 and 3 Nov '14; WO 95/5289, War Diary IEF B, 5 Nov '14, Appendix VII, 'Report on Action at Tanga on 3rd November 1914' by Brig.-Gen. M.J. Tighe, 5 Nov '14. Henceforth, *Tighe Report*.

2. WO 95/5318, War Diary 13th Rajputs, 3 Nov '14.

3. Boell, *Die Operationen*, p.78; WO 95/5289, War Diary IEF B, 5 Nov '14, *Tighe Report*.

4. NAM, 6506/16, Priestland papers, [17 FK] *Gefechtbericht zum 2. und 3. November bei Tanga*,

p.3; NAM 6505/16, Priestland papers, [17 FK], 'The Fight at Tanga'.

5. WO 95/5318, War Diary 13th Rajputs, 3 Nov '14.

6. NAM, 6506/16, Priestland papers, *Gefechtbericht zum 2. und 3. November*, pp.3–4; Boell, *Die Operationen*, p.78. A platoon of *1 FK*, *6 FK* and *6 Sch K*.

7. WO 107/45, *Malleson Report*, pp.2–3.

8. WO 95/5289, War Diary IEF B, 5 Nov '14, *Tighe Report*.

9. WO 95/5339, War Diary 2nd Loyal North Lancashire, 3 Nov '14; Hordern, *Military Operations – East Africa*, pp.82–83.

10. WO 107/45, *Malleson Report*, Appendix A, Notes of Experiences by Lt-Col. C. Bailey, Base Embarkation Commandant, B Force, p.2: Appendix B, Personal Narrative of Lt-Col. R.G. Macpherson, Commandant Base Depot, IEF B, Appendix A, p.1 and Appendix B, p.1. Henceforth, *Malleson Report – Bailey* and *– Macpherson*.

11. WO 95/5289, War Diary IEF B, 5 Nov '14, *Tighe Report*; WO 95/5344, War Diary 61st Pioneers, 8 Nov '14, 'Report on Action at Tanga on 3 November 1914.'

12. WO 107/45, *Malleson Report*, p.4.

13. WO 95/5318, War Diary 13th Rajputs, 3 Nov '14; WO 95/5344, War Diary 61st Pioneers, 3 Nov '14.

14. Boell, *Die Operationen*, p.78 says fire was opened at 0915; ADM 53/42071, Log HMS *Fox*, 3 Nov '14, states that eleven rounds were fired at 1000 hours; she did not anchor in the harbour and despatch beach parties until 0740: Hordern, *Military Operations – East Africa*, writes that fire was opened at 0740; NAM, 6506/16, Priestland papers, *Gefechtbericht zum 2. und 3. November*, pp.3–4 indicates that fire was opened at 0945. It would seem that the firing took place some time between 0900 and 1000 hours.

15. WO 107/45, *Malleson Report*, p.5.

16. WO 107/45, *Malleson Report*, p.6.

17. Hordern, *Military Operations – East Africa*, p.82. The 13th Rajputs were estimated to have five of twelve British officers and forty-nine of 690 other ranks, the 61st had lost two British officers and ninety-one other ranks, of about 400. These represent 7.8% and 23.3% of the engaged strengths.

18. WO 95/5289, War Diary IEF B, 3 Nov '14, message Tighe to Aitken.

19. IWM, 49538, *Schutztruppe KTB*, 3 Nov '14.

20. IWM, 49538, *Schutztruppe KTB*, 3 Nov '14.

21. WO 95/5369, War Diary 3rd Kashmir Rifles, 3 Nov '14.

22. WO 95/5289, War Diary IEF B, 1900 hours, 3 Nov '14.

23. WO 95/5369, War Diary 101st Grenadiers, 3 Nov '14; IWM, 88/61/1, Wapshare papers, Diary, 3 Nov '14.

24. WO 138/41, Gen. Aitken Personnel File, 16 Nov '14, letter Aitken to general [unnamed – presumably Barrow at the India Office], p.3.

25. WO 95/5289, War Diary IEF B, 4 Nov '14; CAB 45/6, *Aitken Account*, Dec '16. The War Diary states landing was completed by 1000 hours while Aitken is rather more circumspect saying 'very early the next morning'; Hordern, *Military Operations – East Africa*, pp.83–84.

26. Boell, *Die Operationen*, p.79; Hauer, *Kumbaki*, p.59; NAM, 6506/16, Priestland papers, *Gefechtbericht zum 2. und 3. November*, p.5.

27. Lettow, *Reminiscences*, pp.38–39.

28. Boell, *Die Operationen*, p.79; Hordern, *Military Operations – East Africa*, pp.530–531.

CHAPTER 7

THE SECOND ATTACK – 4 NOVEMBER 1914

1. Hordern, *Military Operations – East Africa*, pp.97–99.

2. IWM, 49538, *Schutztruppe KTB*, 3 Nov '14.

3. WO 138/41, Gen. Aitken Personnel File, 16 Nov '14, letter Aitken to general [unnamed – presumably Barrow at the India Office], p.3.

4. WO 95/5369, War Diary 101st Grenadiers and 3rd Kashmir Rifles, 4 Nov '14; WO 95/5333, War Diary 98th Infantry, 4 Nov '14.

5. CAB 45/6, *Aitken Account*, Dec '15, pp.10–11.

6. WO 95/5289, War Diary IEF B, 3 Nov 1914.

7. WO 95/5289, War Diary IEF B, 4 Nov '14; Graham, Brig. C.A.L., *The History of the Indian Mountain Artillery*, Aldershot: Gale and Polden, 1957, pp.137–138.

8. CAB 45/6, *Aitken Account*, Dec '15, pp.10–11.

9. WO 95/5369, War Diary 3rd Kashmir Rifles, 4 Nov 1914; WO 95/5339, War Diary 2nd Loyal North Lancashire, 4 Nov 1914.

10. WO 95/5289, War Diary IEF B, 4 Nov '14, Operation Order No. 3.

11. Boell, *Die Operationen*, pp.78–79; Lettow, *Reminiscences*, pp.38–40.

12. WO 95/5333, War Diary 98th Infantry, 'The Action at TANGA, 4 Nov 1914', p.1.

13. IWM, PP/MCR/150, King papers, Diary, 1–4 Nov 1914.

14. NAM, 6506/16, Priestland papers, [*17 FK*] *Gefechtbericht zum 4. November bei Tanga*, p.6; Lettow, *Reminiscences*, pp.39–40.

15. WO 107/45, *Malleson Report*, p.7.

16. WO 95/5941, War Diary 3rd Kashmir Rifles, 'Report on Action 4 November, 1914 at TANGA', pp.2–3;

17. WO 95/5333, War Diary 98th Infantry, 'The Action at TANGA, 4 Nov 1914', p.1.

18. WO 95/5941, War Diary 63rd Palamcottah Light Infantry, 4 Nov '14, 'Report on Tanga'; War Diary 101st Grenadiers, 11 Nov '14, 'Report on the Part Taken by 101st Grenadiers in the Action at Tanga 4 Nov 1914'; WO 95/5339, War Diary 2nd Loyal North Lancashire, 4 Nov '14.

19. WO 95/5941, War Diary 63rd Palamcottah Light Infantry, 12 Nov '14, 'Report of 63rd PLI'.

20. WO 95/5941, War Diary 101st Grenadiers, 11 Nov '14, 'Report of 101st Grenadiers'.

21. IWM, 88/6/1, Wapshare papers, Diary, 4 Nov '14.

22. WO 95/5941, War Diary 3rd Kashmir Rifles, 4 Nov '14, 'Report on Tanga'; WO 95/5318, War Diary 13th Rajputs, 4 Nov '14.

23. Lettow, *Reminiscences*, pp.41–42.

24. Boell, *Die Operationen*, pp.79–80.

25. Zirkel, 'Military Power in German Colonial Policy', p.97.

26. Lettow, *Mein Leben*, pp.121 and 127–128; Schnee, *Ostafrika im Weltkrieg*, p.73; Miller, *Battle for the Bundu*, pp.12–13.

27.   Köhl, Hauptmann Franz, *Der Kampf um Deutsch-Ostafrika*, Berlin: Verlag Kameradschaft, [1919], p.15.

28.   WO 95/5339, War Diary 2nd Loyal North Lancashire, 4 Nov '14.

29.   WO 107/45, *Malleson Report – Bailey*, p.2 and – *Macpherson*, p.2.

30.   NAM, 6506/16, Priestland papers, *Gefechtbericht zum 4. November*, p.7.

31.   WO 95/5333, War Diary 98th Infantry, 4 Nov '14, 'Report on Tanga'; WO 95/5339, War Diary 2nd Loyal North Lancashire, 4 Nov '14; WO 95/5941, War Diary 101st Grenadiers, 4 Nov '14, 'Report on Tanga'.

32.   Dept, *Mit Lettow-Vorbeck Durch Africa*, Berlin: Verlag August Scherl, 1919, p.41; WO 95/5318, War Diary 13th Rajputs, 4 Nov '14

33.   Lettow, *Reminiscences*, p.42.

34.   IWM, PP/MCR/150, King papers, Diary, 1–4 Nov 1914; WO 95/5941, War Diary 101st Grenadiers, 4 Nov '14, 'Report on Tanga'.

35.   WO 158/439, 'Despatch on the Tanga Operations', pp.7–8.

36.   IWM, PP/MCR/150, King papers, Diary entry 1–4 Nov 1914.

37.   CAB 45/6, *Aitken Account*, Dec '15, pp.12–13; IWM, 88/6/1, Wapshare papers, Diary, 4 Nov '14.

38.   NAM, 6506/16, Priestland papers, *Gefechtbericht zum 4. November*, p.8; *2 Aug*, [*17 FK*] *Gefechbericht vom 4. November 1914 bei Tanga*, p.2.

39.   BA/MA, N103/83, 4 Nov 1914, Telegram Aruscha to Umbulu.

CHAPTER 8

THE WITHDRAWAL ON 4 AND 5 NOVEMBER

1.   CAB 45/6, *Aitken Account*, p.2.

2.   IWM, PP/MCR/150, King papers, Diary, 5 Nov 1914; CAB 45/6, *Aitken Account*, p.13.

3.   WO 95/5289, War Diary IEF B, 4 Nov '14, Appendix 14, Telegram S17, Aitken to War Office.

4.   CAB 45/6, *Aitken Account*, p.14.

5.   IWM, PP/MCR/150, King papers, Diary, 5 Nov 1914.

6.   WO 95/5289, War Diary IEF B, 5 Nov '14.

7.   Hordern, *Military Operations – East Africa*, p.93.

8.   IWM, PP/MCR/150, King papers, Diary, 5 Nov 1914; IWM, 77/109/1, Johnson papers, '61st Pioneers, 1914'.

9.   WO 5339, War Diary 2nd Loyal North Lancashire, 5 Nov '14; WO 5289, War Diary IEF B, 5 Nov '14.

10.   Lettow, *Reminiscences*, p.43; Boell, *Die Operationen*, pp.81–82.

11.   ADM 53/42071, Log HMS *Fox*, 5 Nov '14.

12.   Crichton-Harris, Ann, *Seventeen Letters to Tatham*, Toronto: Kennegy West, 2001, pp.52–53. Letter Dr Temple Harris to Tatham Harris, 28 Nov '14.

13.   IWM, 77/109/1, Johnson papers, '61st Pioneers, 1914'; 88/6/1, Wapshare papers, Diary, 5 Nov '14.

14.   WO 95/5289, War Diary IEF B, 5 Nov '14; Hordern, *Military Operations – East Africa*, p.96.

15. IWM 88/6/1, Wapshare papers, Diary, 5 Nov '14; CAB 45/6, *Aitken Account*, pp.13–14.

16. Meinertzhagen, *Army Diary*, pp.98–99.

17. WO 95/5289, War Diary IEF B, 5 Nov '14; Lettow, *Reminiscences*, p.44.

18. WO 157/1112, Intelligence Summary IEF B, 5 Nov 1914.

19. WO 157/1112, Intelligence Summary IEF B, 6 Nov 1914.

20. Lettow, *Reminiscences*, p.43.

21. BA/MA, N103/83, 5 Nov 1914, Telegram Morogoro to Umbulu: Deppe, *Mit Lettow-Vorbeck*, p.44.

22. Hordern, *Military Operations – East Africa*, p.96 for British losses and p.107 for German casualties; Boell, *Die Operationen*, pp.82 and 530–531.

23. Boell, *Die Operationen*, p.82. Company figures are not available.

24. British numbers include all infantry battalions, force and brigade headquarters, brigade signal sections and the field ambulances. The mountain battery and non-combat units, approximately 1,600 men, have been excluded. The German numbers are based on an estimated battle strength of 1,100 and not the final strength of 5 November.

25. Hordern, *Military Operations – East Africa*, p.107; Boell, *Die Operationen*, p.82.

CHAPTER 9

EPILOGUE

1. WO 95/5289, War Diary IEF B, 6 Nov '14, Appendix 24, Telegram 1332, War Office to Aitken.

2. WO 95/5289, War Diary IEF B, 13 Nov '14, Appendix 41, Telegram S38, Aitken to Secretary of State for India; 15 Nov '14, Appendix 51, Telegram 1367, Secretary of State for India to Aitken.

3. WO 95/5289, War Diary IEF B, 20 Nov '14, Appendix 59, Telegram S56, Aitken to Secretary of State for India.

4. WO 95/5289, War Diary IEF B, 22 Nov '14, Appendix 61, Telegram 1396, War Office to Aitken.

5. WO 157/1112, Intelligence Summary IEF B, 6 Nov '14. These claims appear to have come directly from Capt. Meinertzhagen during his two visits to the Germans – although he later disparaged Aitken for accepting his own report, see Meinertzhagen, *Army Diary*, p.104. The numbers of Europeans was greatly exaggerated and with British sea power, the possibility of reservists reaching East Africa by sea was very unlikely. However, the Germans may have been engaged in disinformation or Meinertzhagen confused the reservists with the replacement crew landed from SMS *Planet*. These men were intended to serve in the East Asiatic Squadron, but were diverted to East Africa on the outbreak of war; WO 95/5289, War Diary IEF B, 20 Nov '14, Appendix 36, Telegram S32, Aitken to CGS, Delhi.

6. WO 33/714, European War Secret Telegrams, Series B, 31 July 1914 to 31 January 1915, No. 1320, 22 Nov '14, Telegram 2188, Kitchener to Sir Beauchamp Duff; No. 1339, 23 Nov '14, Telegram 16 S, Duff to Kitchener; No. 1523, 4 Dec '14, Telegram 127, War Office to Aitken.

7. WO 138/41, Aitken Personal File, Minute DCIGS to Secretary of State for India, 5 May '19.

8. CAB 45/6, *Aitken Account*, pp.6–7 and 'Memorandum of the Operations at Tanga" to cover

letter of 31 July '14 [*sic* – note attached to letter of 20 Feb '17].

9.   WO 138/41, Aitken Personal File, Letter Aitken to War Office, 29 Apr '20, p.1.

10.   WO 95/5289, War Diary IEF B, 2 Nov '14.

11.   WO 138/41, Aitken Personal File, 3 Mar '20, Memorandum 'Notes on the Operation Against TANGA', by Deputy Director of Military Operations.

12.   Hordern, *Military Operations – East Africa*, p.101, footnote 1.

13.   WO 138/41, Aitken Personal File, 26 Jan '15, Telegram 36, Admiralty to *Fox*.

14.   WO 138/41, Aitken Personal File, 28 Jan '15, Telegram *Fox* to Admiralty.

15.   WO 138/41, Aitken Personal File, 28 Aug '20, Letter Admiralty to War Office, enclosing statement by Rear Admiral Caulfield [*sic*].

UNPUBLISHED PRIMARY SOURCES

Public Record Office (PRO), Kew, London
    ADM Series
       1 – General
       53 – Ships' Logs
       123 – Station Records Africa
       137– War Orders Admiralty to Foreign Stations
    CAB Series
       5 – Memoranda Colonial Defence
       8 – Colonial and Overseas Defence
       11 – Defence Schemes
       21 – CID Office Registered Files
       44 – Official Histories
       45 – Notes on Official Histories
    WO Series
       33 – Operations and Administration Papers
       95 – War Diaries
       106 – Director of Military Operations/Director of Military Intelligence
       107/45 – Malleson–Cowans Correspondence
       138/41 – Aitken Personal File
    Files
       153 – Maps and Plans
       157 – Intelligence Summaries
       158 – Correspondence and Papers Military Headquarters
       300 – Maps East Africa
Bodlieian Library, Oxford
    Harcourt Papers
Bundesarchiv/Militärarchiv, Freiburg im Breisgau
    Boell Papers (N14)
    von Lettow-Vorbeck Papers (N103)

Imperial War Museum, London

    Cook Papers (P80)

    Hammill Papers (92/18/1)

    Johnson Papers (77/109/1)

    King Papers (PP/MCR/150)

    Schutztruppe Diaries 49538 (4 vols)

    Wapshare Papers (88/6/1)

National Army Museum, London

    Davidson Papers (6112/661)

    Priestland Papers (6506/16)

South African National Defence Force, Documentation Directorate Photographic Archive

Published Primary Sources and Memoirs

Churchill, W.S., *The World Crisis: 1911–1914*, Volume 1, London: Thomas Butterworth Limited, 1923.

Deppe, Ludwig, *Mit Lettow-Vorbeck durch Afrika*, Berlin: Verlag August Scherl, 1919.

Hankey, Lord, *The Supreme Command*, 2 Volumes, London: Allen and Unwin, 1961.

Hauer, Dr August, *Kumbake: Erlebnisse eines Artze in Deutsch-Ostafrika 1914–1919*, Berlin: Hobbing, 1922.

Lloyd George, D, *War Memoirs*, 2 Volumes, London: Odhams Press, 1938.

Keen, Maj. F.S., 'Lecture on the Campaign in East Africa: Delivered at Simla on the 6th October 1916', *Journal of the United Service Institution of India*, XLVI, 1917, pp.71–91.

King-Hall, Adm Sir H.G., *Naval Traditions and Memories*, London,1926.

Köhl, Hauptmann Franz, *Der Kampf um Deutsch-Ostafrika*, Berlin: Verlag Kameradschaft [1919].

Lettow, Gen. Paul von, *My Reminiscences of East Africa*, London: Hurst and Blackett, 1920. Reprinted Nashville, Tennessee: The Battery Press [n.d.].

Lettow-Vorbeck, Gen. Paul Emil von, *Mein Leben*, (ed./pub.) (Herausgegeben von Ursula von Lettow-Vorbeck), Biberach an der Riss: Koehlers, 1957.

Meinertzhagen, Col. R., *Army Diary 1899–1926*, London: Oliver and Boyd, 1960.

Methner, Wilhelm, *Unter drei Gouverneuren: 16 Jahre Dienst in den deutschen Tropen*, Breslau: Korn, 1938.

Oxford and Asquith, Earl of, *Memories and Reflections*, Volume 2, London: Cassell and Co., 1928.

Robertson, Field Marshal Sir William, *Soldiers and Statesmen 1914–1918*, London: Cassell and Co., 1926.

Schnee, Ada, *Meine Erlebnisse während der Kriegszeit in Deutsches Ostafrika*, Leipzig: Quelle und Meyer, 1918.

Schnee, Dr Heinrich, *Deutsch-Ostafrika im Weltkrieg*, Leipzig: Quelle und Meyer, 1919.

Schnee, Dr Heinrich, *Als Letzer Gouverneur in Deutsch-Ostafrika: Erinnerungen*, Heidelberg: Quelle und Meyer, 1964.

Schoenfeld, Fregattenkapitän Werner, *Geraubtes Land: Durchs freie Südafrika ins bedrohte Deutsch-Ostafrika*, Dresden: Deutscher Buch- und Kunstverlag, 1942 (reprint of 1925 original).

Stewart, Sir J.M., *Jimmie Stewart – Frontiersman: The Edited Memoirs of Major General Sir J.M. Stewart,* (ed.) Robert Maxwell, Edinburgh: Pentland Press, 1992.

Wenig, Richard, *In Monsun und Pori*, Berlin: Safari-Verlag, 1922.

Wynne, E., *Ambush*, London: Hutchinson and Co., 1937.

Official Publications

Admiralty, *Review of German Cruiser Warfare 1914–18*, London: HMSO, 1940.

Admiralty (NID), *A Handbook of German East Africa*, London: HMSO, 1923.

Admiralty (NID), *A Handbook of the Uganda Protectorate*, London: HMSO, 1920.

Assmann, Konteradmiral Kurt, *Der Krieg zur See 1914–1918: Die Kaempfe der Kaiserlichen Marine in den Deutschen Kolonien*, Berlin: Verlag E.S. Mittler & Sohn, 1935.

Corbett, Sir Julian S., *History of the Great War: Naval Operations*, I, London: Longmans, Green and Co., 1920.

Hordern, Lt-Col. Charles, *Official History of the Great War: Military Operations: East Africa, 1914–1916*, Volume 1, London: HMSO, 1941.

India Army List, Calcutta: Government of India, 1906–1914.

Lucas, Sir C.P., *The Empire at War: Volume 4: Africa*, Oxford: Oxford University Press, 1925.

Macpherson, Maj.-Gen. Sir W.G. *et al.*, *History of the Great War: Medical Services General History Vol. 1: Medical Services in the United Kingdom; in British Garrisons Overseas; and During Operations against Tsingtau; in Togoland, the Cameroons, and South-West Africa*, London: HMSO, 1921.

Macpherson, Maj.-Gen. Sir W.G. and Mitchell, Maj. T.J., *History of the Great War: Medical Services General History Vol, 4; Medical Services During the Operations on the Gallipoli Peninsula; in Macedonia; in Mesopotamia and North-West Persia; in East Africa; in the Aden Protectorate, and in North Russia: Ambulance Transport During the War*, London: HMSO, 1924.

Raeder, Kapitän zur See E, *Der Krieg zur See 1914–1918, Der Kreuzerkrieg in den ausländischen Gewässern*, I, Berlin: E.S. Mittler & Sohn, 1922.

Raeder, Kapitän zur See E, *Der Krieg zur See 1914–1918, Der Kreuzerkrieg in den ausländischen Gewässern*, II, Berlin: E.S. Mittler & Sohn, 1923.

Reichsarchiv, *Der Weltkrieg 1914 bis 1918: Die Militärischen Operationen zu Lande*: *9. Band*, Berlin: E.S. Mittler & Sohn, 1942.

Russell, Maj. A., 'The Landings at Tanga, 1914', *Tanganyika Notes and Records*, No. 58, Mar/Sep 1962, pp.103.

War Office, *Field Service Regulations, Parts I and II*, London: HMSO, 1909.

Secondary Sources

Anderson, Ross, 'The Battle for Tanga, 2–5 November 1914', *War in History*, 8 (3), 2001.

Andrew, Christopher and Kanya-Forster, *France Abroad*, London: Thames and Hudson, 1981.

Bald, Detlef, *Deutsch-Ostafrika 1900–1914: Eine Studie über Verwaltung Interessengruppen und Wirtschäftliche Erschliessung*, Munich: 1970.

Beesly, P., *Room 40: British Naval Intelligence 1914–1918*, London: Hamilton, 1982.

Bidwell, Shelford and Graham, Dominick, *Fire-Power: British Army Weapons and Theories of War 1904–1945*, London: George Allen & Unwin, 1982.

Body, Capt. O.G., 'Bush and Forest Fighting Against Modern Weapons', *Army Quarterly*, VIII, pp.314–324.

Boell, Ludwig, *Die Operationen in Ostafrika*, Hamburg: Walter Dachert, 1951.

Brose, Eric Dorn, *The Kaiser's Army*, Oxford: Oxford University Press, 1991.

Cocker, Mark, *Richard Meinertzhagen: Soldier, Scientist and Spy*, London: Secker and Warburg, 1989.

Crichton-Harris, Ann, *Seventeen Letters to Tatham*, Toronto: Kennegy West, 2001,

Dane, Edmund, *British Campaigns in Africa and the Pacific 1914–1918*, London: Hodder and Stoughton, 1919.

Eberlie, R.F., 'The German Achievement in East Africa', *Tanganyika Notes and Records*. No. 55 (September 1960), pp.181–213.

Eckart, Wolfgang U., *Medezin und Kolonial-Imperialismus Deutschland 1884–1945*, Paderborn: Schoenigh, 1997.

Farndale, Gen. Sir M., *History of the Royal Artillery: The Forgotten Fronts and the Home Front 1914–1918*, London: The Royal Artillery Institute, 1988.

Fischer, F., *Germany's Aims in the First World War*, London: Chatto and Windus, 1967.

French, David, *British Strategy and War Aims 1914–1916*, London: Unwin and Allen, 1986.

Gann, L.H. and Duignan, P., *The Rulers of German Africa 1884–1914*, Stanford: Stanford University Press, 1977.

Gann, L.H. and Duignan, P., *The Rulers of British Africa 1878–1914*. Stanford: Stanford University Press, 1978.

Gardner, Brian, *German East Africa: the Story of the First World War in East Africa*. London: Cassell, 1967.

Gifford, Prosser and Lewis, William Roger (eds), *Britain and Germany in Africa: Imperial Rivalry and Colonial Rule*, New Haven: Yale University Press, 1967.

Gilbert, Martin, *Winston S. Churchill: Volume III 1914–1916*, London: Heinemann, 1971.

Gilbert, Martin, *Winston S. Churchill: Volume III Companion 2 1914–1916*, London: Heinemann, 1971.

Gooch, John, *The Plans of War: The General Staff and British Military Strategy c.1900–1916*, London: Routledge & Kegan Paul, 1974.

Graham, Brig. C.A.L., *The History of the Indian Mountain Artillery*, Aldershot: Gale and Polden, 1957.

Groener, Erich, *German Warships 1815–1945: Volume I Major Surface Vessels*, Annapolis Md: Naval Institute Press, 1990.

Guinn, Peter, *British Strategy and Politics 1914 to 1918*, Oxford: Clarendon Press, 1965.

Halpern, Paul G., *A Naval History of World War I*, London: UCL Press, 1994.

Hatchell, G.W., 'The East African Campaign: 1914 to 1919', *Tanganyika Notes and Records*, XXI, (June 1946), pp.39–45.

Hauer, August, *Kumbaki: Erlebnisse eines Artze in Deutsch-Ostafrika 1914–1919*, Berlin: Hobbing, 1919.

Haupt, Werner, *Deutschlands Schutzgebietes in Übersee 1884–1918*, Friedberg: Podzun-Pallas-Verlag, 1984.

Hazlehurst, Cameron, 'Asquith as Prime Minister, 1908–1916', *English Historical Review*, LXXXV (1970), pp.502–531.

Heichen, Walter, *Helden der Kolonien: Der Weltkrieg in unseren Schutzgebieten*, Berlin: A. Weichert
    Verlag [n.d.].

Hodges, G.W.T., 'African Manpower Statistics for the British Forces in East Africa, 1914–1918',
    Journal of African History, IX, No. 1 (1977), pp.101–116.

Hodges, Geoffrey, *The Carrier Corps: Military Labour in the East African Campaign*, Westport, Conn:
    Greenwood Press, 1986.

Hoyt, Edwin P., *The Germans Who Never Lost*, New York: Funk & Wagnell's, 1968.

Hoyt, E.P., *Guerrilla: Colonel von Lettow-Vorbeck and Germany's East African Empire*. New York:
    Macmillan, 1981.

Hughes, C. and Nicholson, I.E., 'A Provenance of Proconsuls: British Colonial Governors
    1900–1960', *Journal of Imperial and Commonwealth History*, IV, No. 1 (1977), pp.77–106.

Iliffe, John, *Tanganyika under German Rule 1905–1912*, Cambridge: Cambridge University Press, 1969.

Iliffe, John, *Africans, History of a Continent*, Cambridge: Cambridge University Press, 1995.

Kaponen, Juhani, *German Colonial Policies in Mainland Tanzania 1884–1914*, Studia Historica 49,
    Helsinki: Finnish Historical Society, 1995.

Keble Chatterton, E., *The Königsberg Adventure*, London: Hurst and Blackett, 1936.

Killingray, David, 'Labour Exploitation for Military Campaigns in British Colonial Africa,
    1870–1945', *Journal of Contemporary History*, XXIV, No. 3 (July 1989), pp.483–502.

Langhorne, R.T.B., 'The Anglo-German Negotiations Concerning the Future of the Portuguese
    Colonies in Africa', *Historical Journal*, XVI, No. 2 (1973), pp.361–387.

Lloyd-Jones, *King's African Rifles: Being an Unofficial Account of the Origins and Activities of the KAR*,
    London: Arrowsmith, 1926.

Majumdar, Lt-Col. Birenda, 'Development of the transport system in the Indian Army from 1760 to
    1914', *Army Quarterly*, LXXVII (1959), pp.250–260.

Marder, Arthur, *From the Dreadnought to the Scapa Flow: The Royal Navy in the Fisher Era, 1904–1919*,
    I, Oxford: Oxford University Press, 1961.

Miller, Charles, *The Battle for the Bundu*, London: Macdonald and Jones, 1974.

Mombauer, Annika, *The Origins of the First World War*, London: Longman, 2002.

Mombauer, Annika, *Helmuth von Moltke and the Origins of the First World War*, Cambridge: Cambridge
    University Press, 2001.

Monson, Jamie, 'Relocating "Maji-Maji"', *Journal of African History*, 39, 1998, pp.95–120.

Mosley, Leonard, *Duel for Kilimanjaro*, London: Weidenfeld & Nicolson, 1963.

Moyse-Bartlett, Lt-Col. H., *The King's African Rifles*, Aldershot: Gale and Polden, 1956.

Nalder, Maj.-Gen. R.F.H., *The Royal Corps of Signals: A History of its Antecedents and Development*,
    London: Royal Signals Institution, 1958.

Orr, Col. G.M., 'The Indian Army in East Africa 1914–1917', *Journal of the United Service Institution of
    India*, XLVIII, (1919), pp.244–261.

Orr, Col. G.M., 'Some Afterthoughts of the War in East Africa, 1914–1918', *Journal of the Royal
    United Services Institute*, LXIX (1924), pp.692–702.

Page, Melvin E. (ed.), *Africa and the First World War*, London: Macmillan, 1987.

Patience, Kevin, *Königsberg: A German East African Raider*, Bahrein: Zanzibar Publications, 1997.

Petter, Wolfgang, 'Das Offizierkorps der Deutschen Kolonialtruppen 1889–1918', *Das Deutsche
    Offizerkorps 1860–1960*, ed. Franz, Günther, Boppard am Rhein: Harald Boldt Verlag, 1977,

Ritter, Gerhard (Trans. Heinz Norden), *The Sword and the Sceptre: The Problem of Militarism in Germany, Volume III: The Tragedy of Statesmanship – Bethmann Hollweg as War Chancellor (1914–1917)*. London: Allen Lane, 1973.

Roskill, Stephen, *Hankey: Man of Secrets*, Volume 1, London: Collins, 1970.

Rothwell, V.F., *British War Aims and Peace Diplomacy 1914–1918*, Oxford: Oxford University Press, 1971.

Sands, Lt-Col. E.W.C., *The Indian Sappers and Miners*, Chatham: Institution of Royal Engineers, 1948.

Savage, Donald C. and Forbes Munro, J., 'Carrier Corps Recruitment in the British East Africa Protectorate, 1914–1918', *Journal of African History*, VII, No. 2 (1966), pp.313–342.

Sheppard, Brig.-Gen. S.H., 'Some Notes on Tactics in the East African Campaign', *Journal of the United Service Institution of India*, XLVIII, No. 215 (April 1919), pp.138–157.

Singh, Maj. K. Brahma, *History of Jammu and Kashmir Rifles 1820–1956*, New Delhi: Lancer International, 1990.

Solf, Wilhelm, 'Schnee und von Lettow-Vorbeck', *Die Deutsche Nation* (1920), pp.87–95.

Strachan, H.F.A., *The First World War – To Arms*, Volume I, Oxford: Oxford University Press, 2001.

Stone, Glyn A, 'The Official British Attitude to the Anglo-Portuguese Alliance, 1910–1945', *The Journal of Contemporary History*, X, No. 4, October 1975, pp.729–748.

Stronge, Capt. H.C.T., 'Bush Warfare Against Trained Troops', *Journal of the Royal United Services Institution*, LXXII, (1927), pp.603–613.

Stoecker, Helmuth (ed.) (Bernd Zoellner, trans.), *German Imperialism in Africa: From the Beginnings until the Second World War*, London: C. Hurst & Co., 1986.

Taute, Dr M., 'A German Account of the Medical Side of the War in East Africa, 1914–1918', *Tanganyika Notes and Records*, VIII (December 1939), pp.1–20.

Turner, J., 'Cabinets, Committees and Secretariats: The Higher Direction of War', in K.M. Burk (ed.), *War and State: The Transformation of British Government 1914–1918*, London: George Allen & Unwin, 1982, pp.57–83.

Vincent-Smith, J.D., 'The Anglo-German Negotiations over the Portuguese Colonies in Africa, 1911–14', *The Historical Journal*, XVII, No. 3, 1974, pp.620–629.

Vincent Smith, J.D., 'Britain, Portugal and the First World War, 1914–1918', *European Studies Review*, IV, No. 3 (1974), pp.207–238.

Vincent Smith, J.D., 'The Portuguese Republic and Britain, 1910–1914', *Journal of Contemporary History*, X, No. 4 (1975), pp.707–727.

Wock, H.W., *The Story of the Congo Free State*, New York: Putnam, 1905.

Woodhouse, Capt. H.L., 'East Africa', *Journal of the United Service Institution of India*, XLVI (1917), pp.329–337.

Woodward, D.R., 'Britain in a Continental War: The Civil Military Debate over the Strategical Direction of the War of 1914–1918', *Albion*, XII (1980), pp.37–65.

Yearwood, Peter J. 'Great Britain and the Repartition of Africa 1914–19', *Journal of Imperial and Commonwealth History*, XVIII, No. 3, (October 1990), pp.316–341.

Wylly, H.C., *The Loyal North Lancashire Regiment*, London: Royal United Service Institution, 1933.

Wynne, Wynn E., *Ambush*, London: Hutchinson and Co., 1937.

Zirkel, Kirsten, 'Military Power in German Colonial Policy', in *Guardians of Empire*, ed. Killingroy, David and Omissi, David, Manchester: Manchester University Press, 1999.

INDEX

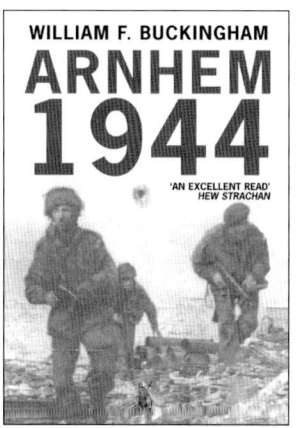